DR. DARRELL PARSONS

Emerging as an
Innovative
Business Leader

10 COMMON CORES FOR MOBILIZING YOUR INFLUENCE INTO THE FUTURE

GLE Books
Virginia USA

Emerging as an Innovative Business Leader—10 Common Cores for
Mobilizing Your Influence into the Future
by Dr. Darrell J. Parsons

GLE Books
an imprint of Parsons Publishing House
P. O. Box 488
Stafford, VA 22555 USA
www.ParsonsPublishingHouse.com
Info@ParsonsPublishingHouse.com

ISBN -13: 978-1-60273-085-4
ISBN -10: 160273-085-7
Printed in the United States of America.
For World-Wide Distribution.

Also available in trade paper.
ISBN -13: 978-1-60273-078-4
ISBN -10: 160273-074-1

TABLE OF CONTENTS

Emerging as an Innovative Leader

Introduction

"If you always do what you always did,
you will always get what you always got."
—Albert Einstein

"Our wretched species is so made that those
who walk on the well-trodden path always
throw stones at those who are showing a new road."
—Voltaire

"Change is the law of life. And those who look only to the
past or present are certain to miss the future."
—John F. Kennedy

The value of an idea is a powerful thing, and the seed-bed for ideas is found in wisdom and understanding. Creating value ties wisdom and knowledge to innovation. According to Oster, the key to creating value in a specific product, service, idea, or process is innovation, which provides a steady stream of new products to businesses competing in a global marketplace (Oster, 2011, p. 16). Innovation may be the key to what many organizations will look like in the future.

Innovation can even save lives. Stop and think about some of the creative and innovative ideas of this modern era. Imagine Rip Van Wrinkle waking up in today's modern society of digital natives and real time information flow. However, innovation is not limited to modern societies with technological enhancements. Innovation can also exist in the deepest jungles and the most remote parts of the world. Ideas can change the world, or, as in Modupe's case, save the known world.

Modupe, whose name means "I am grateful", lived in a village in the deepest part of Africa, where the people made their living by farming. The village lay in a large green valley that was lined with palm trees and bushes. Surrounding the village were fields dotted with crops of yams, cassava, corn, and other vegetables. Just beyond the fields was a deep river that the villagers called Baba, which means father. The river was a friend and a provider for the people: the men used it for fishing, the women washed clothes on its banks, and the children played in its waters. But in the rainy season, the river overflowed, and the people were fearful of its power. So, at a place where the river wound beyond the fields, they built a strong dam to hold back the water.

Modupe was a shy, quiet man whose wife had died and whose children were all married, so he had moved to the top of the mountain overlooking the valley and lived alone. There he had built a small hut and cleared a small piece of land to grow his vegetables. The people did not see Modupe often, but they loved and respected him because he had the gift of healing the sick and because he was one of them.

One year at harvest time, there were unusually heavy rains, but the crops had done well, and there was much to do. No one paid it any mind. As Modupe stood by his home on the mountain, he noticed that the river had become swollen from the rains and was straining the dam. He knew that by the time he could run down to the village to warn the people of the flood, it would be too late and all would be lost. Even as Modupe watched, the wall of the dam began to break, and water started to seep through.

Modupe thought of his friends in the village. Their crops, their homes, and their very lives were in danger if he did not find a way to warn them. Then an idea came to him: he rushed to his small hut and set it afire. When the people of the valley saw Modupe's house burning, they said, "Our friend is in trouble. Let's sound the alarm and go up to help him." Then, according to custom, men, women, and children ran up the mountain to see what they could do. When they reached the top of the hill, they did not have time to ask what had happened—a loud crashing noise behind them made them turn around and look down into the valley. Their house, their temple, and their crops were being destroyed by the river, which had broken the dam and was flooding the valley.

The people began to cry and moan at their loss, but Modupe comforted them. "Don't worry," he said. "My crops are still here. We can share them while we build a new village." Then all the people began to sing and give thanks because they remembered that in coming to help a friend, they had saved themselves (Kouzes & Posner, 1993). Adapted from Nguzo Saba Films Teacher's Guide of film "Ujima" (San Francisco: Nguzo Saba Films) as reported in Friends Can Be Good Medicine (Sacramento, Calif.: California Department of Mental Health, 1981): 58-59.

The Laws of Change

Many times, ideas become the catalyst of change and change becomes the catalyst for innovation. Change is all around us. Seasons are constantly changing. Children are continuously growing and maturing. Relationships are always expanding. Even our bodies are constantly changing over time. Over 2500 years ago, Heraclitus recognized and concluded that nothing endures, but change. Change is everywhere, and the Laws of Change can be synthesized from the Laws of Thermodynamics.

The Thermodynamics of Change

Change requires an energy force in order for it to be lasting and beneficial. The First Law of Thermodynamics basically states that energy cannot be created or destroyed, but converted from one form to another. Therefore, the First Law of Change would be that change cannot be created or destroyed, but converted to work with you or against you. For example, shaping change can propel you into the future or anchor you to the past; wisdom comes in utilizing change to fulfill your purposes. The Second

Law of Thermodynamics states that a system left to itself will tend to decay and become chaotic. The Second Law of Change would be that change must be reviewed and addressed or the organization will tend to decay and become obsolete. For example, a cutting-edge organization will sense the winds of change long before they are felt; whether in the product line or the administration of it, keeping up with the times is essential. The Third Law of Thermodynamics claims that all processes and movements cease as temperature approaches absolute zero. The paradox of this law is that absolute zero is not attainable. This would lead to the Third Law of Change which would state that change will only cease at absolute zero which cannot be achieved, so change is ever-present and always at work. Much like the Law of Gravity, change is ever-present and always at work regardless of the ability to see it.

Competition and Change

Competition is the very bedrock upon which we have built our free-market economy. While competition may be good for an external economic society, it is not always a good internal process for organizational change. Many organizations focus on some type of competitive reward program to create incentives for change or improvement. For example, the most sales this quarter wins a free trip. While this idea might sound good on the surface, competition inside an organization tends to isolate and drive people apart. Deming concludes that competition represents the forces of destruction that comes from the present style of reward for change found in most organizations today; whereas, a cooperative environment preserves the power of intrinsic motivation, dignity, innovative curiosity, and the joy of learning (Deming, 1994). Cooperation is a great enabler for success.

Cooperation and Change

Have you ever been caught in a rip current? The key to surviving a rip current that is pulling someone out to the ocean is not to resist and fight against the current, but to work with the current and swim parallel to the coast. Change, like rip currents, can quickly develop in an organization. To resist and compete against a rip current is to struggle against the odds and possibly even lose the battle. The swimmer must flow and work with the rip current and utilize that energy to be successful. Since the Laws of Change identify that change is all around and constantly at work, the successful organization will work to use the energy of change to be successful rather than resist and compete against it. Cooperative change is about working with the current flow of change in order to produce a more effective and efficient organization. Innovation becomes a product of flowing with change as ideas surface throughout the organization.

The Key to Successful Change is Continuous Improvement

So, the question becomes how does a leader cooperate and use the energy of change for the good of the organization? The key to working with the continual process of change is to develop a mindset or a culture for continuous improvement. Competition only serves to drive people into isolation whereas cooperation is designed to bring people together. Noted author Dr. Stephen Covey identifies the principles of creative cooperation in his sixth habit of highly effective people, which is the habit of synergy (Covey, 1989). Buckminster Fuller, neo-futuristic architect and systems theorist, refined the definition of synergy to mean that the sum of the total is greater than the individual components (Fuller, 1975, p. 102). Simply stated, working together is better than working against or apart. The culture of continuous improvement allows everyone in the organization to work together to manage the energy of change for the good of the organization allowing innovation to surface. For example, in Washington DC, the Pentagon employs close to 24,000 people and has implemented a new security program utilizing those 24,000 pairs of eyes called, *"If You See Something—Say Something."* The strength of incorporating 24,000 people into a security conscious program is incredible. Everyone has ownership of this process and has readily adopted this new program change of heightened alert.

Kaizen

The concept of continuous improvement is not a new idea. It has been around for many years with success stories from around the globe. The Kaizen Institute at *http://us.kaizen.com* is one of many organizations promoting and teaching the concept of continuous improvement. ***Kaizen*** is a Japanese word that means "improvement" or "change for the better" and refers to the philosophy that focuses upon the continuous improvement of processes in manufacturing, engineering, game development, and business management. It has been applied in healthcare, psychotherapy, life-coaching, government, banking, and other industries. When used in the business sense and applied to the workplace, *kaizen* refers to activities that continually improve all functions, and involves all employees from the CEO to the assembly line workers.

This is not a top-down program. Bennis concludes that the idea of all successful change originating from top-down leadership is wrong, unrealistic, and maladaptive as well as potentially dangerous because it is based on the myth of the triumphant individual (Bennis, 2000). Kaizen is a cooperative program that is based upon the concept of continuous improvement. The Toyota Motor Corporation implemented the doctrine of kaizen or continuous improvement for every employee and applies it relentlessly as well as liberally across the corporation. One example is that Toyota offers a cash bonus to employees that can solve production glitches and one particular solved glitch resulted in slashing 75% of the cost of retrofitting the production line, which has saves billions of dollars annually (Daft, 2007).

No Man is an Island

As John Donne said, "No man is an island, entire of itself; every man is a piece of the continent, a part of the main." Transitioning from a competitive environment to a cooperative environment empowers people to take ownership of the change process and allows their gifts and talents to become vital assets to corporate worth. Dr. Bruce Winston from Regent University advocates placing people where their skills, abilities, and spiritual gifts best match the requirements of the position because this is where each person can best serve the organization (Winston B., 2002). According to Dr. John Kotter, many organizations have a leadership deficit because the organization ignores the leadership potential in the members of that organization, thereby, not offering training or relevant role models to raise up leaders from within (Kotter, 2005). Adopting a culture of continuous improvement throughout an organization, unleashes the stored resources of everyone involved in managing and implementing any change process. It also breeds individual ownership of the program, and a sense of fulfillment and contribution to the overall success.

A Common Core of Competencies for Innovative Leaders

Change and innovation work hand-in-hand. Few would argue against the notion that today's modern society is in the midst of a series of crises. However, that point of agreement is quickly lost in the search for solutions. One side claims to have the solutions while another side states that only they have the real answers. Confusion lies in the middle. Part of this confusion can be alleviated by identifying a common core of competencies for emerging innovative leaders. While much of the literature is focused on innovation, very little has been written about a common core of competencies. As an approach to organizational development, innovation leadership can be used to support the achievement of the mission or vision of an organization or group. In a world that is ever changing with new technologies and processes, it is becoming necessary for organizations to think innovatively in order to ensure their continued success and stay competitive. Emerging innovative leaders can begin the process of innovative leadership development by working on the following ten common core competencies:

1. Creativity
2. Strategic Mindset
3. Redesign
4. Trust & Ethics
5. Context
6. Forecasting
7. Rest & Renewal
8. Leadership Succession
9. Mentoring/Discipling
10. Understanding People

Essentially, the innovative leader must think and act as both an inspired, creative genius and the innovative general manager. According to research at Penn State University, innovative leaders must alternate among (Hunter, Steinberg, & Taylor, 2012):

- Facilitating broad, creative thinking about what is possible
- Bringing disparate ideas and consumer insights together into revolutionary product/service ideas
- Analyzing the business risk, financial return, and operational implications of taking the product to market
- Motivating a cross-functional team to collaborate
- Building support throughout the organization

Clearly, this role requires a resiliency to accept ambiguity and to toy with, reframe, and even abandon some ideas.

Without innovative leadership, organizations are more likely to struggle (McEntire & Greene-Shortridge, 2011). This new call for developing innovative leaders represents the shift from the 20th century, traditional view of organizational practices, which discouraged innovative behaviors, to the 21st century view of valuing innovative thinking as a potentially powerful influence on organizational performance (Mumford, Scott, Gaddis, & Strange, 2002).

Leadership is at the core of most successful ventures. However, what is at the core of the leader makes all the difference. Moral failures in leaders seem to be rampant in our modern society. Businesses are closing their doors in record numbers. The housing market is still in a crisis, and the value of the dollar has plummeted. Leaders are being pressed on all sides to produce answers and results. Effective cost and production ideas seem hard to come by today. What many people see as problems, innovative leaders see as opportunities.

Until now, the qualities of leadership that can successfully take a company into the future have been vague and ethereal. Success has been attributed to individuals with timing, or just at the right place, or with certain characteristics that only few "special" people will ever possess. It's time to solidify the once vague attributes and focus a plan on how to create leaders that are needed today and tomorrow. However, where do innovative leaders come from? What are the competencies or qualities of developing an innovative leader?

This book begins the dialogue of identifying distinguishing qualities or competencies to develop innovative leaders. The list is not comprehensive, but at least, identifies a starting point to begin the process for emerging leaders to develop in the quest to become an innovative leader. According to Rothwell, competency models are essential building blocks on which to begin a successful leadership framework (Rothwell, 2005, p. 83). Let's begin.

Chapter 1
The Emerging Innovative Leader

"All men by nature desire knowledge."
—Aristotle

"We cannot solve problems by using the same kind of thinking
we used when we created them."
—Albert Einstein

"I cannot help fearing that men may reach a point where they look on every
new theory as a danger, every innovation as a toilsome trouble, every social
advance as a first step toward revolution, and that they may absolutely
refuse to move at all."
—Alexis de Tocqueville

The single most critical factor in the success or failure of an organization is leadership and that the leader's effectiveness is measured by the success of the organization (Bass B., 2008, p. 11). The integrated definition of leadership provided by Winston and Patterson tie the leaders' ability to select, equip, train, and influence followers directly to a coordinated effort to achieve the organizational mission and objectives (Winston & Patterson, 2006):

> A leader is one or more people who selects, equips, trains, and
> influences one or more follower(s) who have diverse gifts,
> abilities, and skills and focuses the follower(s) to the
> organization's mission and objectives causing the follower(s) to

willingly and enthusiastically expend spiritual, emotional, and physical energy in a concerted coordinated effort to achieve the organizational mission and objectives. The leader achieves this influence by humbly conveying a prophetic vision of the future in clear terms that resonates with the follower(s) beliefs and values in such a way that the follower(s) can understand and interpret the future into present-time action steps. In this process, the leader presents the prophetic vision in contrast to the present status of the organization and through the use of critical thinking skills, insight, intuition, and the use of both persuasive rhetoric and interpersonal communication including both active listening and positive discourse, facilitates and draws forth the opinions and beliefs of the followers such that the followers move through ambiguity toward clarity of understanding and shared insight that results in influencing the follower(s) to see and accept the future state of the organization as a desirable condition worth committing personal and corporate resources toward its achievement. The leader achieves this using ethical means and seeks the greater good of the follower(s) in the process of action steps such that the follower(s) is/are better off (including the personal development of the follower as well as emotional and physical healing of the follower) as a result of the interaction with the leader. The leader achieves this same state for his/her own self as a leader, as he/she seeks personal growth, renewal, regeneration, and increased stamina—mental, physical, emotional, and spiritual—through the leader-follower interactions.

According to Northouse, leadership occurs when others begin to recognize and look towards an individual in the group, regardless of the any title, as becoming the most influential member of the group or organization; this type of leadership occurs over time and is called emergent leadership (Northouse, 2007, p. 5). The development of the emergent innovative leader becomes vital to the continual success of the organization.

Diversity Strengthens Emerging Innovative Leader

One of the many challenges for innovative leadership development is to cultivate an emergent innovative leader that is able to transcend cultures and be effective in today's multi-cultural environment. According to Shahin and Wright, most leadership theories come from North America and may not be applicable across diverse cultures and ethnic groups which differ from the American culture (Shahin & Wright, 2004). As far back as 1993, researchers were highlighting that the current emphasis on management was primarily an American invention and that many other nations practice an entirely different form of management, which needs to be understood (Hofstede G., 1993). Additionally, research indicates that integrating cultural diversity change into leadership development can help companies better develop leaders' strengths to improve aspects of culture within a specific department or the overall company, which will further guarantee that leaders are fully focused on achieving organizational goals (Emerald Group Publishing, 2011). Cultural integration becomes a vital component to the development of emergent innovative leaders and needs to be integrated into the basic leadership theories.

Three Basic Theories

According to Bass, three basic theories can be used to explain how anyone can become leaders (Bass B., 1990). Since these theories were designed to identify basic theories on leadership development, they would also apply to the developing of the emergent innovative leader. These theories are:

1. The Trait Theory: Certain personality traits may lead people naturally into leadership roles.
2. The Great Events Theory: A crisis or important event may cause a person to rise to the occasion and develop/exhibit extraordinary leadership qualities in an ordinary person.
3. The Transformational or Process Leadership Theory: Individuals choose to become leaders and, therefore, learn leadership skills.

The Trait Theory

The trait theory is also known as the Great-Man Theory. Colorful phrases such as "he was born to lead" and "she is a natural leader" are used to identify this theory. Bass reports that these theories draw attention to specific qualities of leaders and until the 1940's much of the research about leadership focused on these individual traits (Bass B., 2008, p. 49). Theorists identify many historical leaders under this heading; for example, without Moses, the children of Israel would have remained in Egypt and without Winston Churchill, the British would have surrendered in 1940 (Bass B., 2008, p. 48).

The Great Event Theory

The great events theory is also known as situational theories, which is dependent upon the concept that leadership is a matter of situational demands, and these situational factors will determine who emerges as a leader; this theory is in direct opposition to the traits theory and is particularly favored in the Unites States (Bass B., 2008, p. 52). Other research also calls this theory the momentous event theory which introduces personal uncertainty into the relational structure of the leader and describes momentous events as distinctive, circumscribed, and highly emotional (Olivares, 2011). Pillemer defines momentous events as follows (Pillemer, 2011):

- The memory represents a specific event that took place at a particular time and place.
- It contains a detailed account of the person's own personal circumstances at the time; the memory includes sensory imagery (visual, auditory, olfactory, or tactile).
- The "rememberer" believes that the event actually happened.

President George W. Bush responds to the momentous event of the terrorist attacks on 911, and no other attack occurs during his presidency.

The Transformational Theory

The transformational or process leadership theory is among the new theories of leadership development. For the empirical study of leadership, transformational leadership was a new paradigm or a change of views that was first formalized as a theory by James Burns in 1978 (Bass B., 2008, p. 50). According to Burns, the transforming leader looks for potential motives in followers, seeks to satisfy higher needs, and engages the full person of the follower to result in a mutual relationship that converts followers into leaders (Burns, 1978, p. 4). Bass also defines transformational leadership in terms of how the leader affects followers, who are intended to trust, admire and respect the transformational leader when he identified three ways in which leaders transform followers (Bass B., 2008, p. 50):

- Increasing their awareness of task importance and value
- Getting them to focus first on team or organizational goals, rather than their own interests
- Activating their higher-order needs

Transformational Leadership

Burns defines a transformational leader as one who raises the followers' level of consciousness about the importance and value of outcomes and how to effectively reach them (Burns, 1978). The obvious emphasis is upon the followers. Bass concludes that transformational leadership is about changing people and transformational leaders motivate their followers to do more than they originally intended or thought possible (Bass B., 2008).

Many transformational leaders are also charismatic in nature. Khurana issues a caution concerning charismatic-only leaders when he states that the charismatic succession process implies that a single individual deserves vastly more attention and rewards than anyone else in the organization, and ignores the reality that organizational performance is driven by more than one person (Khurana, 2002, p. 197). Bass relates the dynamics of the charismatic leader-follower relationship and concludes that charismatic leaders often use themselves as examples for their subordinates to follow

(Bass B., 2008, p. 590). Northouse identifies four specific types of charismatic behavior (Northouse, 2007, pp. 178-179):

- They are strong role models for the beliefs and values they want their followers to adopt.
- They appear competent to followers.
- They articulate ideological goals that have moral overtones.
- They communicate high expectations for followers and they exhibit confidence in their followers' abilities to meet these expectations.

The study of transformational and charismatic leadership is relatively recent, but the research has been steadily growing. Burns first introduced the transforming leader in 1978 when he concluded that transforming leadership was best built upon a relationship of mutual stimulation and elevation that converts followers into leaders and leaders into moral agents (Burns, 1978). While charismatic leadership can be regarded as part of transformational leadership, some research indicates that the undesirable consequences at the societal level of charismatic leadership include totalitarian aspects as well as truth manipulation practiced by some charismatic leaders (Aaltio-Marjosola & Takala, 2000).

Servant Leadership

It is also important to distinguish servant leadership from transformation leadership. According to Stone, Russell and Patterson, transformational leaders direct their focus toward the organization, so their behavior builds follower commitment toward organizational objectives, while servant leaders focus on their followers, and the achievement of organizational objectives is a subordinate outcome (Stone, Russell, & Patterson, 2004). Kotter concludes that many organizations have a leadership deficit because the organization ignores the leadership potential in the members of that organization, thereby, not offering training or relevant role models to raise up leaders from within (Kotter, 2005). Deming outlines three steps to get others involved in accomplishing transformative change (Deming, 1994):

- The transformative leader has a theory and understands why the transformation would bring gains to the organization as well as the people involved in the organization.
- The transformative leader feels compelled to accomplish the transformation as an obligation to the people and the organization.
- The transformative leader has a step-by-step plan and can explain it in simple terms.

A transformational leader can make the organization more successful by valuing its human capital. Northouse determined that the effect of organizational change through transformational leaders is the ability of the transformational leader to be a role model, create a vision and empower followers to facilitate ownership of the process (Northouse, 2007). However, transformational leadership is not just a North American concept. From a cross-cultural perspective, Dr. Y.L.J. Lam from the Chinese University of Hong Kong concludes that transformational leadership is a very effective type of leadership in many cultural settings (Lam, 2002). Bass identifies that charismatics can foster antisocial behavior, and personalized charismatic leaders can be dominant, self-interested, and authoritarian (Bass B., 2008, p. 578). While charismatic and transformational leadership styles are similar, there are some differences; especially when measured against the servant leadership style.

Transformational leadership is considered by many to be closest to the "prototype" of leadership that people have in mind when they describe an ideal leader which is more likely to provide a role model with which followers want to identify as well as emulate (Bass B., 2008, p. 51). Bass calls this the identification process in his characteristics of leaders as leaders and followers begin to identify with one another to produce a collective identity (Bass B., 2008, p. 589).

Create an Identification Culture

The Walt Disney Company would be an example of this identification process. When Walt Disney was alive he was completely engaged in creating the Disney culture. However, Walt Disney suddenly dies and the company has to decide who was going to continue the culture of creation.

After weeks of deliberation, the Disney Company decided that Walt Disney was still going to be used to create the culture. All the executives who worked personally with Walt Disney gathered together and began to write down all the things that they could remember that Walt would do and say. From this workshop, the Traditions Course was developed and every cast member of the Disney organization is required to attend this course including the current Chief Executive Officer (Disney Institute, 2001, pp. 11-13). Since Walt Disney created the Disney culture, he would be the one to continue producing this culture long after he was gone.

Emerging innovative leaders can learn about the need to be persuasive and motivational to their followers from this example. As organizations grow, new leaders are constantly stepping up to positions of authority. These leaders can come from within the organization as long as the organization is taking the time to develop, train and mentor these new leaders. Since the goal of the identification process is persuasion and motivation, organizations that promote from within will demonstrate that focused work for the group good will be rewarded. Many times, other organizations will persuade some of the best talent to leave one company for another. One of the best arguments to stay with a company is the knowledge that the company has your best interests in mind when you have the company's best interests in mind. Promotion can come from internally instead of moving around from company to company. Bass states that leaders should work to include the worth of the individual to produce a collective history and a productive future (Bass B., 2008, p. 589)

Create an Identification Culture

The Walt Disney Company would be an example of this identification process. When Walt Disney was alive he was completely engaged in creating the Disney culture. However, Walt Disney suddenly dies and the company has to decide who was going to continue the culture of creation. After weeks of deliberation, the Disney Company decided that Walt Disney was still going to be used to create the culture. All the executives who worked personally with Walt Disney gathered together and began to write down all the things that they could remember that Walt would do and say. From this workshop, the Traditions Course was developed and every cast member of the Disney organization is required to attend this course including the current Chief Executive Officer (Disney Institute, 2001, pp. 11-13). Since Walt Disney created the Disney culture, he would be the one to continue producing this culture long after he was gone.

Emerging innovative leaders can learn about the need to be persuasive and motivational to their followers from this example. As organizations grow, new leaders are constantly stepping up to positions of authority. These leaders can come from within the organization as long as the organization is taking the time to develop, train and mentor these new leaders. Since the goal of the identification process is persuasion and motivation, organizations that promote from within will demonstrate that focused work for the group good will be rewarded. Many times, other organizations will persuade some of the best talent to leave one company for another. One of the best arguments to stay with a company is the knowledge that the company has your best interests in mind when you have the company's best interests in mind. Promotion can come from internally instead of moving around from company to company. Bass states that leaders should work to include the worth of the individual to produce a collective history and a productive future (Bass B. , 2008, p. 589).

Common Language and a Common Vocabulary

Developing a common language and a common vocabulary for the identification process can produce profound results. This process is called a narration. A narration reflects the voice or voices through which the words of the text speak (Robbins, 1996, p. 15). This pattern moves the discourse forward. Emerging innovative leaders understand the need to build and develop a proper narration because it sets the stage in broader terms than just the daily routine of work. Whether the company is a large organization or a small business, day-in day-out work can become mundane and trivial. However, as the company sets the stage for how that work is being used to promote a greater good and to support a greater cause, the followers and the leaders can begin to see the bigger picture. Bass explains that eloquence and rhetoric are vital to the development of a leaders' team (Bass B. , 2008,

p. 586). Miller concludes that every leader leads through the process of team building, and all leaders need a narrative structure for their vision or it will lose its definition and purpose (Miller, 1995, pp. 68, 166).

Complete the Narration

As a finishing touch to the narration, add the sensory-aesthetic pattern, which is associated with the senses of thought, emotion, sight, sound, touch, and smell along with their interaction (Robbins, 1996, pp. 29-30). Typically, these patterns can be described as three types of zones; the zone of self-expressive speech, the zone of emotion-fused thought, and the zone of purposeful action. This is where passion and purpose become paramount. Yet, many leaders do not fully understand how passion and purpose interact. Passion is not an emotional response to an event. Passion is the product of a released purpose. Once purpose is understood and uncovered, passion becomes the fuel to move the organization forward. Any organization that lacks passion is the product of misaligned or misunderstood purpose. A properly developed narration, that is used to reveal purpose, will produce passion.

Emerging innovative leaders can implement this in the roles of leaders and followers as they use verbal and nonverbal cues to interact together. Leaders and followers need to be able to articulate their feelings and emotions to one another to learn interdependence. Bass identifies these types of patterns as expressive behavior and insight (Bass B., 2008, pp. 584-585).

The use of the identification process and the corresponding narrative can keep the organization on a path toward success. As purpose and passion flow through an organization, creativity is unleashed.

Chapter 2
The Common Core of Creativity

"Everybody born comes from the Creator trailing wisps of glory. We come from the Creator with creativity. I think that each one of us is born with creativity."
—Maya Angelou

"A discovery is said to be an accident meeting a prepared mind."
—Albert Szent-Gyorgyi

Creativity and innovation have also been around since the beginning of time. While technologies may change over time, creativity and innovation provide the catalyst for the next technological event.

The First Goal of Creativity

The first goal for creativity and innovation should be to tap into an unlimited resource. Michalko concludes that creativity is decided by what people choose to do and what they refuse to do (Michalko, Thinkertoys, 2006, p. xv). To release creativity requires seeing something different than everyone else. Albert Szent-Györgyi, a Hungarian-born biochemist who won the Nobel Prize in 1937, stated that creativity and discovery consist of seeing what everybody has seen and thinking what nobody has thought (Szent-Gyorgyi, 1962). According to Oster, creativity requires a careful tending process and everyone must be absolutely sure that wild and unusual ideas are welcomed as well as ensuring that any impediments to creativity are removed (Oster, 2011, pp. 18-19).

The Greatest Challenge to Creativity

Perhaps the greatest challenge to releasing creativity is the stifling of the creative process that is required to think innovatively. Businesses where creativity is not valued and nurtured will struggle to compete with more visionary enterprises because innovative leadership requires creativity in order to produce effective results (Strategic Direction, 2008). Cooper contends that creativity plays a vital role in the innovative thinking process in order to produce a sustained competitive advantage but also admits that many organizations actually discourage the freedom of practicing creativity (Cooper, 1998). Oster concludes that creative thinkers and innovators never seem to be corporate insiders much less those on the organizational fast track and many times they need organizational cover from corporate fire since they do everything possible to escape the shackles of precedent, tradition, and orthodoxy (Oster, 2011, pp. 236-237). According to Gryskiewicz, creativity and innovation have been found to be the cornerstone of healthy organizations that are ready for reinventing themselves, and organizations accomplish this by being relevant to changing markets as well as the use of new technology (Gryskiewicz, 1999, p. 1).

When Einstein was asked to identify the difference between himself and an average person, he responded that an average person looking for a needle in a haystack would stop looking after finding the needle, but he (Einstein) would continue to look through the entire haystack to find all the needles (Michalko, Cracking Creativity, 2001, p. 3). Today's leaders can create environments that facilitate and encourage employee creativity by empowering collaboration through the sharing of tacit knowledge. Oguz and Sengün contend that tacit knowledge as a concept has its origins in Michael Polanyi's writings whose aim was to bring forward the inarticulate dimension of human knowing (Oguz & Sengün, 2011). Tacit knowledge can be a source of a huge range of opportunities and potentials that constitute discovery and creativity as employees must be given the time, space and opportunity to transfer and, therefore, share tacit knowledge which is transmitted verbally (Seidler-de Alwis & Evi, 2008). This sharing becomes a key enabler of collaboration. According to Stagich, leaders in the new millennium must understand how to work successfully in collaborations across nationalities and cultures (Stagich, 2006, Kindle Locations 89-92).

Zweifel determines that global leaders, managers, and entrepreneurs must also become global citizens that will know what gifts to bring to dinner in Singapore as well as how to run a consensus-building meeting in Germany (Zweifel, 2003, p. 75). Von Krough et al. conclude that tacit knowledge is the most important source of creativity, yet it is often underutilized in an organization and difficult to separate from productive work (Von Krogh, Ichijo, & Nonaka, 2000, p. 176). Branson from the Australian Catholic University affirms the need to develop a more human organization that meets the needs of the people in the organization by paying attention to their sense of self and organizational leaders need to restore the meaning of work by involving workers collaboratively in decisions that affect them personally and professionally (Branson, 2009, p. 108). As workers collaborate, this inarticulate dimension of human knowing is shared and encouraged throughout the organization.

Creativity Gaps

Sanchez-Bueno and Suarez-Gonzalez postulate that some new organizational forms may create a fundamental gap between the characteristics of the traditional organizational structures with the more innovative organizational form, and this gap may produce a non-innovative result (Sanchez-Bueno & Suarez-Gonzalez, 2010). This type of gap and non-innovative result actually happened to the Walt Disney Company. After Walt Disney's untimely death in 1966, his son-in-law assumes the CEO responsibilities and attempts to reorganize and realign the Walt Disney Company to make it more modern and up-to-date (Gabler, 2007). However, the innovative culture of the Disney Company begins to deteriorate after Walt's death because of a gap in the creative culture that Walt Disney developed and his successor changed (Thomas, 1994). As a reminder, the leadership of the Walt Disney Company also developed a program called "Traditions" to impart the importance of the Disney culture, heritage, values and policies as originally taught by Walt Disney to close the creative gap (Disney Institute, 2001).

Roy Disney Jr. (Walt's nephew) successfully led the Board of Directors to replace Walt Disney's son-in-law as the CEO with Michael Eisner who had to take the Traditions course on his first day of employment (Eisner, 1999). Eisner immediately re-established much of the organizational structure that Walt Disney used to enhance creativity. As Eisner began to merge Walt Disney's innovative culture with his own innovative culture and ideas, the Walt Disney Company expanded well beyond its previous boundaries in productivity and profit (Gabler, 2007). Eisner brought with him a vast background of experiences from his work at Paramount and ABC which he used to rebuild the Disney culture of innovation (Thomas, 1994). Eisner has come and gone at Disney, but the Traditions course is still a requirement for every cast member including the current Disney CEO (Gabler, 2007).

Pre-Emptive Crisis Management

In order to build and sustain an organizational culture dominated by creativity and innovation, learning organizations must effectively identify and mobilize the creative resources of their members before the intrusion of a crisis. Research at the London School of Economics define a learning organization as one that is able to change its behaviors/mind-sets as a result of experience, which may sound like an obvious statement, yet many organizations refuse to acknowledge certain truths or facts and repeat dysfunctional behaviors over and over again (Mitleton-Kelly, 2013). Tushman and O'Reilly claim that all too frequently organizational change is the product of crisis conditions, but the more successful firms do not wait until a crisis occurs before proactively developing/solving problems (Tushman & O'Reilly, 2002, p. 40).

Pro-active leadership development can help resolve a situation before a crisis can develop. Covey concludes that the ability to pause and then choose the response is the key to being proactive rather than reactive (Covey, 1989, p. 71). Creativity and innovation are critically important for organizations seeking to survive and thrive in today's highly turbulent business environments, and leadership development may represent one important key for unlocking this idle creative potential and enhancing overall organizational effectiveness (Houghton & DiLiello, 2010). One element of leadership development across learning organizations can be the emphasis upon everyone in the organization being creative. According to van Woerkum et al. from the Communication Management Group, Wageningen University, The Netherlands, being creative should be a part of an organization's everyday experiences, a component of normal meetings, and a reality for all members of an organization (van Woerkum, Aarts, & de Grip, 2007). Unlocking creativity and innovation before it is needed, will help learning organizations pre-empt a crisis situation.

The First Step

Perhaps the first step in the creative process could be to start asking "what's next". Gryskiewicz states that growth, creativity and stretching can be developed from the "what's next" question (Gryskiewicz, 1999, p. 52). Tushman and O'Reilly claim that all too frequently organizational change is the product of crisis conditions but the more successful firms do not wait until a crisis occurs before proactively developing or solving problems (Tushman & O'Reilly, 2002, p. 40). Bass contends that leaders need to be intuitive about what comes next and try to make it happen (Bass B. , 2008, p. 688). In order to build and sustain an organizational culture dominated by creativity, learning organizations must effectively identify and mobilize the creative resources of their members before the intrusion of a crisis. Developing a creative culture is not necessarily complex and most organizations can begin developing the creative culture at any time. Tushman and O'Reilly further explain that creativity only requires two main ingredients (Tushman & O'Reilly, 2002, p. 113):

- Support for Risk Taking
- Tolerance for Mistakes

Nadler and Tushman contend that much of the actual discussion on organizational structure does not show up on any formal charts, but it is centered in the ideologies, political alliances, collective self-images, webs of influence, career expectations, and patterns of behavior, which identifies what has come to be known as the "soft stuff" of organizational management and structure (Nadler & Tushman, 1997, p. 194). Creativity lies somewhere hidden in this "soft stuff" waiting to be discovered.

Discovering and utilizing combined creativity in the "soft stuff" of an organization will allow a person to renovate and produce a complete change for the better.

Creativity that Abides

Creativity is considered to be the source of new and competitive ideas through which an organization positions itself in its environment and, in rapidly changing conditions, organizations must meet the challenge of being capable of creating tomorrow's business while maintaining today's (van Woerkum, Aarts, & de Grip, 2007). Houghton and DiLiello define creativity as the process of forming novel, useful and appropriate ideas in order to solve problems and increase effectiveness, and view creativity as an individual or team level process; while innovation involves the successful implementation of creative ideas at the organizational level (Houghton & DiLiello, 2010). Although heavily influenced by their history and culture, organizations that develop an inter-dependence can transcend both when necessary, and they are able to explore the space of possibilities and find a different way of doing things, i.e., they are creative and innovative and can create something new (Mitleton-Kelly, 2013).

Education and technology are excellent keys for learning organizations to develop creativity. Tushman and O'Reilly notes that even Apple had to eventually expand and grow through education and technological advancements (Tushman & O'Reilly, 2002, p. 24). With tighter budgets and a global context, many educational and technological institutions are struggling to remain relevant for today and tomorrow. Canton states that innovation investments will be the key trend that will promote future leadership, education, quality of life, and global competitive advantages (Canton, 2006). The 2012 Horizon Report on higher education from the New Media Consortium identifies a timeline for technology implementation: one year or less for Mobile Apps and Tablet Computing; two to three years for game-based learning and learning analytics; four to five years for gesture-based computing (New Media Consortium, 2012). Additionally, the United Kingdom Government wants over 50% of their young people going to a university, and will rely on distance learning to meet this goal (Grocock, 2002). These trends and events would set the stage for non-traditional career paths led by creativity and technology innovations.

The global demand for higher education is likely to reach 160 million by 2025 with India and China becoming the two largest countries seeking higher education, and the demand is growing at the rate of 20% per annum in India (Gupta, 2008). Additionally, the New Media Consortium identifies the top 3 trends in higher education for 2012-2017 (New Media Consortium, 2012):

- People will expect to be able to work, learn, and study whenever and wherever they want and life in an increasingly busy world will produce more mobile students.
- Technologies will become increasingly cloud-based, as people are growing accustomed to a model of browser-based software that is device independent.
- The world of work will increasingly become more collaborative in nature and to facilitate more teamwork and group communication, projects will rely on tools such as wikis, Google Docs, and Skype.

According to Schneider and Littrell, many characteristics of the German way of management may be traced back to their national education system and its strengths in engineering, technical training and craft as well as German culture being less individualistic than the Anglo-Saxons; therefore the build-up of a long-term cooperative partnership between owners, managers and workers find a more fertile ground (Schneider & Littrell, 2003). Tushman and O'Reilly provide the success story of the turn-around of British Airways and conclude that their competitive advantage was the product of a cooperative shared culture throughout the organization that led to an increase in creativity and innovation (Tushman & O'Reilly, 2002, p. 33). To create an organization with a creative framework that abides requires a cooperative mindset to permeate throughout the entire organization. Everyone's involvement is paramount to producing a creative culture that abides. This type of creative thinking begins the process of developing a global strategic mindset.

Emerging as an Innovative Business Leader

Chapter 3
The Common Core of a Strategic Mindset

"Strategy without tactics is the slowest route to victory.
Tactics without strategy is the noise before defeat."
—Sun Tzu

"Would you tell me which way I ought to go from here?" asked Alice.
"That depends a good deal on where you want to get," said the Cat.
"I really don't care where" replied Alice.
"Then it doesn't much matter which way you go," said the Cat.
—Lewis Carroll

Strategic leadership is a topic that comes and goes in the course of the lives of most leaders. Innovative leaders are usually expected to provide answers and solutions to set the course for the future of their group or organization. Successful innovative leadership can be difficult to achieve because it does not follow a set pattern or form for each and every company or organization. However, there are some key elements that can be identified to assist leaders in developing a course of action in getting more of their people involved in innovative leadership, which will produce a strategic mindset for the people as a whole and the organization in particular. Two of these key elements are strategic thinking and strategic planning. Strategic, or simply strategy, becomes the common word for each of these key elements. Strategy is not a new concept. It has been around for literally thousands of years.

Sun Tzu and 2500 Years of Strategy

Strategy is a pattern that has demonstrated consistency in behavior over time and is applicable across all areas in industry (Mintzberg, Ahlstrand, & Lampel, 2005). Perhaps one of the oldest books ever written on the topic of strategy is *The Art of War* which is a 7000 word "book" originally written on bamboo strips around 500 B.C. by the master strategist Sun Tzu (Michaelson, 2001). Even after 2500 years of consistency over time, Sun Tzu is still relevant for military, government and business strategic leadership lessons. Many of the present day business strategies of organizations can be found in the foundational work of Sun Tzu (Oliver, 1999). A study in Hong Kong by Ho and Sculli conclude that the strategic guidance of Sun Tzu is not only applicable in a Chinese management structure but in all studies of strategy covered in management science (Ho & Sculli, 1998).

However, strategy is a difficult word to define because strategy is always used within a context of competition and change which can best be described like nailing Jell-O™ to a wall (Marren, 2010). Mintzberg et al. identify five definitions related to strategy and determine that strategy is a word that is defined one way but used in a different manner; he also produced 10 schools of thought on strategy (Mintzberg, Ahlstrand, & Lampel, 2005):

1. The Design School, which sees strategic management as a process of attaining a fit between the internal capabilities and external possibilities of an organization.
2. The Planning School, which extols the virtues of formal strategic planning and arms itself with SWOT analyses and checklists.
3. The Positioning School, heavily influenced by the ideas of Michael Porter, which stresses that strategy depends on the positioning of the firm in the market and within its industry.
4. The Entrepreneurial School, which emphasizes the central role played by the leader.
5. The Cognitive School, which looks inwards into the minds of strategists.

6. The Learning School, which sees strategy as an emergent process —strategies emerge as people come to learn about a situation as well as their organization's capability of dealing with it.
7. The Power School, which views strategy emerging out of power games within the organization and outside it.
8. The Cultural School, which views strategy formation as a process rooted in the social force of culture.
9. The Environmental School, which believes that a firm's strategy depends on events in the environment and the company's reaction to them.
10. The Configuration School, which views strategy as a process of transforming the organization—it describes the relative stability of strategy, interrupted by occasional and dramatic leaps to new ones.

De Kluyver defines strategy as the act of positioning a company for competitive advantage by focusing on unique ways to create value for customers (de Kluyver & Pearce II, 2012). Innovation leadership would greatly benefit from the study of strategic thinking and strategic planning by Sun Tzu and even Clausewitz.

Clausewitz

Many times, strategy indicates a military context. Military leaders have been using the strategic teachings of Clausewitz since his widow published his famous book **On War** in 1832 and no true strategist can fully understand the complexities of strategy without delving into Clausewitz (The Strategy Institute of the Boston Consulting Group, 2001). According to Oliver, many of the present day business strategies of organizations can be found in the foundational work of Clausewitz and Sun Tzu (Oliver, 1999). Clausewitz may be best known for his "fog of war" concept, which is used to describe the uncertainty in situational awareness activities experienced by participants in military operations but would also apply to uncertainty in any strategic endeavor.

Strategic Thinking

Strategy has also been defined as a learning process and a strategic mindset can be defined as a way of thinking about how to craft and implement that learning process (Hughes & Beatty, 2005). As more people across the organization get involved, sustainability becomes a greater possibility. The world is becoming increasingly "flat," which means that to effectively conduct business in this new world it will require a different kind of leader; a leader who will not only have to be generally effective in the traditional skills expected, but also with additional knowledge, skills and, above all, a mindset to navigate through the complexities brought on by moving beyond one's traditional borders (Cohen S. L., 2010).

Successful leaders working in complex, ambiguous or chaotic environments think more strategically than less successful leaders in those same environments. Three cognitive processes associated with strategic thinking can be identified as potential distinguishers between successful leaders and less successful leaders: reflection, systems thinking, and reframing (Pisapia, Reyes-Guerra, & Coukos-Semmel, 2005).

Reflection

Reflection is a cognitive skill that involves careful consideration of any belief or practice that promotes understanding of situations and then applying newly gained knowledge to these situations (Pisapia, Reyes-Guerra, & Coukos-Semmel, 2005). It relies on subjecting evidence, perception and experience to critical scrutiny in order to make sense and meaning of situations prior to weaving the thinking into a theory of practice. By reflecting on both successes and failures, leaders begin to unpack the assumptions and values that lie beneath rules, regulations and processes in work and everyday life. This constant effort of reevaluation and interpretation is an integral part of how leaders make sense of situations.

Systems Thinking

Systems thinking rests on the notion that the "whole is greater than the parts." In systems thinking the whole is primary and the parts are secondary. When developing a global strategic mindset, this level of strategic thinking focuses on the big picture concept. In other words, start with the forest as a whole and then spiral down into the individual trees.

Systems thinking are invaluable in a cause and effect analogy. This is especially important in strategic thinking as it pertains to future development and insight, which allows modeling a change in the system in order to predict a series of outcomes.

Reframing

Leaders frame and place all situations in a context. Framing is a cognitive process that helps us gather and organize information and create knowledge. It involves sorting and interpreting the meaning of new information, events, and experiences. Framing imposes assumptions and provides a language for analysis of behavior in which certain aspects of situations are chosen to be considered and interpreted. Reframing has grown in importance since the mid-1980s and Morgan contends that situations and/or problems could be framed and reframed in different ways allowing new kinds of solutions to emerge (Morgan, 1997, p. 337).

Strategic Thinking Leads to Strategic Planning

While the first element or component of developing a strategic mindset involves strategic thinking, it also leads to the second component, which is strategic planning. Even Sun Tzu made reference to a Director of Strategic Planning (Michaelson, 2001). Strategic thinking and strategic planning are interrelated processes and both are necessary for effective strategic management (Heracleos, 1998). However, strategic planning comes after strategic thinking and involves writing or updating a written plan. It requires the clear setting of goals and objectives which are then used to provide the organization with its core priorities as well as a set of written guidelines for virtually all day-to-day managerial decisions (Harrison, 1995). Mintzberg concludes that strategic planning establishes and formularizes systems and procedures (Mintzberg, 1994).

Producing a Strategic Mindset

In every organization, leaders struggle with meeting the demands of a globalized society and local constraints. During the latter half of the last century, leadership challenges were largely framed in the cold war context that created a stabilizing and linear notion of change. Today, the stability of all institutions is challenged by the rapid speed of change driven by globalization, shifting populations, integration of advanced information, and communications technologies which diminishes the impact of time, space, and distance. This transition from the modern industrial age to the postmodern information age with its accompanying complexity is creating a profound challenge for all organizational leaders (Pisapia, Reyes-Guerra, & Coukos-Semmel, 2005).

In today's globally connected society, traditional leaders and leadership structures are becoming a thing of the past. Many organizations are becoming flatter and leadership styles more flexible. According to Bennis, today's globally connected organizations are evolving into federations, networks, clusters, cross-functional teams, temporary systems, ad hoc task forces, lattices, modules, matrices—almost anything but pyramids with their obsolete top-down leadership (Bennis, 1999). A globally connected society requires globally connected leaders. McCall and Hollenbeck identified seven competencies for a global strategic leader (McCall Jr. & Hollenbeck, 2002, p. 36):

- Open Minded and Flexible in Thought and Tactics
- Cultural Interest and Sensitivity
- Able to Deal with Complexity
- Resilient, Resourceful, Optimistic and Energetic
- Honesty and Integrity
- Stable Personal Life
- Value-Added Technical or Business Skills

Time and experience become the true measures of these competencies for innovative leaders. This becomes a greater challenge for globally connected leaders and organizations. However, starting with these seven competencies is a step in the right direction.

Synthesis of Strategic Thinking and Planning

Strategic thinking and planning involves synthesis, which encourages intuitive, innovative and creative thinking (Mintzberg, Ahlstrand, &

Lampel, 2005). From the field of education, Benjamin Bloom identifies six levels of thinking, which are commonly called Bloom's Taxonomy of Learning. Synthesis and evaluation are the fifth and sixth level of Bloom's Taxonomy. According to Bloom, "synthesis" is the ability to put ideas together, propose plans, form solutions, and create new information; whereas, in the "evaluation" stage, the thinker is able to make choices, select, evaluate and make judgments about information and situations (Bloom, 1971). Bloom further contends that in order to get to this level, cognitive thought processes must go through the other four levels which consist of knowledge, comprehension, application and analysis (Bloom, 1971).

In other words, for strategic thinking to work at the synthesis level of thinking, the accumulation of facts and knowledge must lead to a comprehensive understanding which leads to an application and analysis process. Then, the level of synthesis in the strategic thinking process can begin. Strategic planning is closely related to Bloom's evaluation level where choices are selected, acted upon, and then evaluated. Hughes and Beatty emphasize that strategic thinking and strategic planning lead to strategic acting and strategic influence (Hughes & Beatty, 2005). This thought carries out Bloom's evaluation level of thinking. This type of processing becomes more circular than linear. Evaluations are made which may lead back to the need for more facts and knowledge, and the cycle of continuous improvement continues.

Strategic thinking is focused on conceptualizing alternatives and choices through vision and innovation. It leads to the clear setting of goals and objectives which are then used to provide the organization with its core priorities as well as a set of written guidelines for virtually all day-to-day managerial decisions (Harrison, 1995). Where strategic thinking is conceptual of the vision, strategic planning involves writing the vision. While it may seem easy to confuse the difference between thinking and planning, the distinction can be found in that thinking is based on conceptualizing and planning is based upon the writing of goals and objectives to be followed. Thinking precedes planning and planning makes the thinking process actionable. This type of planning works for countries as well as organizations.

Global Use of Strategic Thinking

All countries including developing countries can benefit from strategic thinking. Many global organizations struggle with finding answers to the questions about the needs of the present and what to do about the needs of tomorrow. Mintzberg et al. state that one of the seven deadly sins of strategic planning is to neglect the organizational and cultural requirements of strategy (Mintzberg, Ahlstrand, & Lampel, 2005). Like organizations, successful countries and cultures are dependent upon strategic leadership and strategic thinking. Hughes and Beatty identify five strategic thinking competencies that can be used for organizations or countries: scanning, visioning, reframing, making common sense and systems thinking (Hughes & Beatty, 2005).

Leadership of a country in a complex world that is ever changing and becoming more competitive can especially benefit from the systems thinking component. Palaima and Skaržauskiene reported in the *Baltic Journal of Management* that effective decision making in a world of growing dynamic complexity requires leaders to become systems thinkers in order to develop tools to understand the structures of complex systems that make up in the inner workings of any culture (Palaima & Skaržauskiene, 2010). Some countries are still struggling to make adaptation to a global environment surrounded by complex systems. The Sudan, especially in the Darfur region, provides an example of a failed state due to poor governance, institutional failures in the country as whole, the failure of economic institutions and the breakdown of local institutions (Madichie, 2011). With tribal factions and local juntas fighting for control in the failed state of Sudan, the concept of strategic thinking is not at work. A stable government may be the first step in order to begin building a nation with the five components of strategic thinking. This is also true for organizations. When an organization is in crisis mode, strategic thinking is usually one of the first items dropped from consideration. It is difficult to plan for long-term goals and objectives when the ship is sinking.

According to Yaprak and Sheldon, political risk assessment must be considered, and integrating political risk management into the corporate planning function of a multinational firm is required, in order to produce a successful strategic plan for investment into a country and identified several events in the Middle East and North Africa to demonstrate the volatility of global political currents of the day (Yaprak & Sheldon, 1984). It is of interest to note that even though this article was written in 1984, many of the same type of events are currently taking place in those same areas today.

Frynas references that many business managers and strategic planners identify the political instability in Africa as a key obstacle to its economic development (Frynas, 1998). Additionally, the United Nations identifies that in many developing countries one of the primary challenges for strategic planning and growth is the need for political stability (United Nations, 2006). Mintzberg et al. conclude that strategy formation is a process of social interaction based upon the beliefs and understandings that are shared by the members of an organization (Mintzberg, Ahlstrand, & Lampel, 2005). Successful social interaction to develop a strategic plan is difficult at best in a dictatorship regime or a politically unstable government/ environment. While political stability may not be the primary factor in a countries' strategic plan development, political risk assessment is an important component of a country or cultural group developing a successful strategic plan.

According to Hans Finzel, failure to focus on the future is one of the top ten mistakes that leaders make and concludes that vision is an effective leader's chief preoccupation (Finzel, 1994). Bennis identifies that the key to a leader moving into the future is to develop a mental image that articulates a view of a realistic yet credible and attractive future for the organization (Bennis W. G., 1992). Sanders determines that pictures and images have the power to convey content and meaning and that visualization is the key to both insight and foresight which leads to the next revolution in strategic thinking and planning (Sanders T. I., 1998). While different countries or cultures may vary in the implementation of the strategic plan, visual thinking and producing an achievable vision would seem to be a vital step during the strategic thinking process. Oster concludes that a vision which is extraordinarily expansive and even unreasonable—many would say impossible—is the key to producing successful innovation (Oster, 2011). Not all strategic plans lead to innovation. Visual thinking can still be used in the innovation process. The ability to see beyond the realistic and peer into the impossible or near impossible requires a leader to push beyond the edge to see what may be out there.

Go Global Act Local

A global mindset is vital for innovative leaders of today. One option for global leaders to create environments that facilitate and encourage employee creativity could be to look for local experts. Von Krough et al. state that managers should assign local experts or spokespeople to the knowledge that is dispatched (Von Krogh, Ichijo, & Nonaka, 2000, p. 218). Global leaders must also consider local cultural components. To engage with people of other cultures requires the leader to travel and stay in those areas in order to learn about the people, their cultures and ideologies.

According to Robbins, the Ideological Texture begins with people, and he defines ideology as an integrated system of beliefs, assumptions, and values (Robbins, 1996, p. 96). DeSilva identifies that Ideological Texture recognizes that a text is not just a vehicle for ideas but rather a vehicle by which the author hopes to achieve a certain goal (DeSilva, 2004, p. 25). Energy and passion are vital for organizational leaders to reach across cultures and build a community. While complex and more gelatinous than Jell-O, strategic thinking and strategic planning will allow innovative leaders to build the core competency of a strategic mindset.

Chapter 4
The Common Core of Redesign

"Never doubt that a small group of thoughtful,
committed, citizens can change the world. Indeed,
it is the only thing that ever has."
—Margaret Mead

"The only person who likes change is a wet baby."
—Mark Twain

Change is everywhere. The status quo no longer exists. Many formerly successful businesses and organizations are closing their doors on a regular basis. Successful organizations of today must keep moving forward looking for new competitive advantages. Many times, what is missing about the dynamics of change is the big picture context in which decisions are made (Sanders T. I., 1998, p. 11). Strategic leadership helps provide that big picture context for organizations. As stated, Hughes and Beatty define strategic leadership as when people think, act, and influence in ways that promote a sustainable competitive advantage for the organization (Hughes & Beatty, 2005, p. 9). People and sustainable become key words in this definition. Future successful organizations need to get more of their people involved in strategic leadership at all organizational levels and functions. As more people begin to see opportunities to work in specific ways that affect the direction and momentum of the organization, they begin to take ownership and leadership of their particular area. The more that people get involved, the more sustainable the strategic leadership plan becomes especially during a time of change and redesign.

Change and Motivation

In today's turbulent environment of organizations, change has become synonymous with standard business practices involving long-term organizational ends which must be reformulated on an ongoing basis; however, the largest barrier to change is not changes to technologies or work processes but changes that involve people (Appelbaum, St-Pierre, & Glavas, 1998). Motivation becomes a key component in enabling changes that involve people inside an organization. If people want the change or at least understand the need for change, there is much less resistance. Deming identifies two types of motivation: intrinsic, which involves the natural inclination to learn and the desire to be around other people whereas extrinsic involves external forces in building self-esteem and motivation (Deming, 1994). However, Deming also concludes that some extrinsic motivation can be used to help build self-esteem, but total submission to external motivation leads to the destruction of the individual (Deming, 1994).

Being part of a successful group is a motivational plan that empowers the people in that group to reach out and recruit others. After all, everybody likes to be on the winning side. However, occasions exist where top-down directed change has met with resistance to produce unfavorable outcomes. For example, the United States Air Force has an unpaid civilian auxiliary component called the Civil Air Patrol (CAP), which used to wear Air Force (AF) uniforms when performing search and rescue missions looking for downed aircraft. After some CAP members did not properly wear the uniform, the AF instituted a top-down uniform change making the CAP uniform more distinct from the AF uniform. However, CAP members affirm that they were motivated solely by a desire to perform the CAP's mission and not motivated by wearing AF uniforms, quit and withdrew commitment. Cheng claims that the AF's misunderstanding of volunteer motivation and the symbolism of organizational uniforms led to a dysfunctional organizational change (Cheng, 1998).

Business processes change over time and in order to reflect new and emerging business needs, the organizational structure often needs to be redesigned. This includes the organizational chart, positional changes, job descriptions, career paths, succession plans, etc. Some organizational redesign is compartmental in an organization while other redesigns are for the organization as a whole. It is one thing to pull out a piece of paper and design a new organizational chart. It is quite another thing to build the right organization for the right reasons, staff it appropriately, and then determine what is required to make that new organization work. Organizations often redesign themselves to unlock latent value and typically pay a great deal of attention to the form of the new design because a successfully implemented redesign is supposed to generate value as well as increasing competitive advantage (Ghislanzoni, Heidari-Robinson, & Jermiin, December 2010). The concept of managing change can also be called redesign, and a successful redesign starts with a well-developed strategic plan.

Redesign Change: A Competitive Advantage

Hughes and Beatty contend that strategic thinking is the collection, interpretation, generation, and evaluation of information and ideas in order to create a competitive advantage for the group or organization (Hughes & Beatty, 2005, p. 44). Businesses where creative thinking is not valued and nurtured will struggle to compete with more visionary enterprises because strategic leadership requires creative thinking and innovation in order to produce effective results (Vaitheeswaran, 2008). Mintzberg's first school of thought is the Design School which sees strategic management as a process of attaining a fit between the internal capabilities and external possibilities of an organization (The Executive Fast Track, 2012):

- This school sees strategy formation as a process of conception.
- Approach: Clear and unique strategies are formulated in a deliberate process. In this process, the internal situation of the organization is matched to the external situation of the environment.
- Basis: Architecture as a metaphor.
- In short: Fit! "Establish Fit!"
- Contributions: Order. Reduced ambiguity. Simplicity. Useful in relatively stable environments. It supports strong, visionary leadership.

- Limitations: Simplification may distort reality. Strategy has many variables and is inherently complex. Bypassing learning. Inflexible. Weak in fast changing environment. There is the risk of resistance (not-invented-here behavior).
- Typical/compare: SWOT Analysis I Ashridge Mission Model

Additionally, organizational growth requires companies to closely monitor their return on investments and return on assets with the Economic Value Added (EVA) and the Market Value Added measures. Lehn and Makhija identified that EVA is employed by a large number of firms, including Coca-Cola, AT&T, Quaker Oats, Eli Lilly, Georgia Pacific, and Tenneco and, unlike traditional accounting measures of performance, EVA attempts to measure the value that firms create or destroy by subtracting a capital charge from the returns they generate on invested capital (Lehn & Makhija, 1996). Creating and identifying value is vital to the success and growth of any company.

Redesign: Innovation

Change brings about restructuring and reorganization: change to the working relationships, change to roles and tasks—plus the personal change relating to all of those organizational changes. Reorganizations are hard work. Organizational redesign can be a traumatic experience for all involved, and may falter as managers lose focus or try to compromise on tough decisions. To be successful, a redesign must be based on sound organizational analysis and an agreed-to, implementable long-term business strategy. The skills that come into play to help formulate and guide future strategy are not just learned from textbooks; they are developed over years of exposure to a broad variety of corporate situations in a wide range of industrial, market and geographical contexts. These qualitative shifts revolutionize our ways of thinking, entailing a radical overhaul of concepts, attitudes and values. It follows that education and training must also change, to meet the demands of a culture in which innovation becomes the universal norm (Garavan & Deegan, 1995). Ashkenas et al. conclude that success factors in the twenty-first century include speed, flexibility, integration and innovation, which is in addition to the traditional success factors of size, role, definition, specialization and control (Ashkenas, Ulrich, Jick, & Kerr, 2002, p. xviii).

Redesign: Seven Factors

With tighter budgets and a global context, many organizations are struggling to stay relevant for today and tomorrow. Innovation may become the key to what many organizational structures and facilities will look like in the future. According to Oster, innovation is defined as the intentional development of a specific product, service, idea, process or environment for the creation of value (Oster, 2011, p. 16). For organizations to remain relevant in an ever-changing society, the value of the product needs to increase. The need to increase product value can lead to structural redesign. However, knowing when to redesign becomes a vital component for the future of organizational development. Nadler and Tushman identify seven factors that push organizations toward redesign (Nadler & Tushman, 1997, pp. 207-216):

1. Patterns of Industry Evolution
    a. Stage 1: Emerging Industries which represents the early days of an organization. These organizations learn from trial and error and quickly innovate on the run.
    b. Stage 2: Evolving Industries represents a time of increased demand. With increasing complexity, size and volume comes the need for more professional management than the original entrepreneurial organization could provide.
    c. Stage 3: Mature Industries occurs as demands level off, which may result in the basis of competition shifts. These organizations become firmly focused on cost, efficiencies and process innovation.
2. Discontinuous Change: Periods of disequilibrium that tend to cause a radical shift away from the status quo.
3. New Structural Materials: Emerges over time leading to the development of new organizational architectures, and as growth accelerates many organizations adopt the new structure which compels other organizations to, at least, give serious thought to revamping their own design. While innovation may weave in and

out of many, if not all, of these factors, it becomes a critical piece of the new structural materials factor. New advances in technology, information, and organizational architecture emerge over time and lead to the development of new organizational structures.

4. Organizational Growth: As organizations grow they don't just get bigger, they get more complex as expansion inevitably brings more volume, more differentiation, more specialization, a broader range of offerings to customers, and new geographic locations.

5. The Success Syndrome: Occurs when companies sow the seed of their own failure in a self-destructive pattern which can occur as organizations increase in size and form bureaucracies to impose rigid controls at the expense of speed and flexibility.

6. Management Succession: The installation of a new CEO often provides the stimulus for major redesign efforts and generally falls into one of the four following categories:
   a. Responding to an inherited crisis
   b. Making a personal statement
   c. Pursuing a new strategy
   d. Shaking up the place

7. Organizational Mutation: At most organizations, there are always some design experiments in the works. Every so often, one of these innovations catches on and, in turn, influences the larger organization design. At these junctures, the gradual evolution of the organization's architecture is jolted by a sudden mutation that accelerates change or steers it in a new direction.

Redesign: World Vision

World Vision is a great example of a not-for-profit humanitarian organization that is reliant upon a unique organizational structure for success and exhibits the Organizational Growth factor. According to Foreman, World Vision International is the current organizational structure of the World Vision Partnership which operates today as a federation of interdependent national offices with three different levels of central control, which are (Foreman, 1999):

- National offices which are under strong central control and are registered in the host country as a branch of World Vision International.
- Intermediate stage national offices that have their own board but have agreed to seek approval from World Vision International for critical management decisions.
- Interdependently national registered offices that are autonomous in internal decision but are expected to coordinate with World Vision International and are bound to the Covenant of Partnership.

The idea for World Vision began in the late 1940's when a war correspondent, Dr. Bob Pierce, was sent to China and his heart was broken due to the need of a single little girl whom he started supporting by sending a monthly amount of money to a local missionary for her care (Irvine, 1996, p. 187). From this meager beginning, World Vision has grown to work in over 90 countries, with an estimated 40,000 employees and volunteers as well as annual revenue close to 3 billion dollars (World Vision, 2012). A solitary encounter with a single individual has produced a global outreach organization.

Redesign: Disney

Another great success story of the modern era is the Walt Disney Company. This example demonstrates many of these seven factors; especially, the Organizational Growth and Management Succession factors. The success of Disney is well known with millions of people visiting Disney theme parks on 3 continents, 4 cruise ships, countless movies. The Walt Disney Company had annual revenue of US $36 billion in 2010 (sec.gov, 2010). What is not as well known is that prior to moving to California, Walt Disney started an animation studio in Kansas City called Laugh-O-Gram Studio in 1922, and had as many as 4 animators working for him including life-long Disney animator, Ub Iwerks (Gabler, 2007, p. 73). However, Walt Disney was never good at handling money so that studio went bankrupt, and Walt Disney moved to California to start Walt Disney Productions with his brother, Roy Disney, taking over as the money manager (Thomas, 1994, p. 75). After successfully starting Walt

Disney Studios, Walt Disney was asked about his key to success; a good failure was his quick response (Thomas, 1994, p. 77). Walt Disney was able to take what he had learned from his failed business venture in Kansas and use that knowledge to make adjustments for the Walt Disney Studios in California.

While, it may be easier to learn from successes, perhaps the greatest amount of learning can come from failures. From their research in Sweden, Politis and Gabrielsson conclude that previous start up experience and the experience from closing down a business are associated with a more positive attitude towards failure (Gabrielsson & Politis, 2009). Walt Disney was well known to state that "It is good to have a hard failure while you are young because it teaches you so much. For one thing it makes you aware that such a thing can happen to anybody, and once you've lived through the worst, you're never quite as vulnerable afterwards (Smith, 2001, p. 32)." After the death of Walt Disney, the leadership of the Walt Disney Company developed a program called "Traditions" which imparts the importance of Disney culture, heritage, values and policies as originally taught by Walt Disney, and part of that class still teaches Walt Disney's belief about having a hard failure (Disney Institute, 2001, p. 32). Mintzberg et al. would call the strategic approach that Walt Disney used as the Entrepreneurial School which sees strategy formation as a visionary process and identifies the CEO as the architect of the strategy (Mintzberg, Ahlstrand, & Lampel, p. 104). After Walt Disney unexpectedly died in 1966, the leadership of the Walt Disney Company developed a program called "Traditions" to impart the importance of the Disney culture, heritage, values and policies as originally taught by Walt Disney (Disney Institute, 2001, p. 84). With the Traditions class firmly in place and currently taught to every employee (called cast members) on their first day at work, including their new CEO, the visionary process of Walt Disney continues even after a hard failure.

Many large organizations will initiate a redesign by making a CEO change in order to recover an organization. The Walt Disney Company is also an example of a large organization that changed the CEO in order to change the culture of innovation of the company. The innovative culture of the Disney Company begins to deteriorate after Walt's death (Thomas, 1994,

p. 354). In order to facilitate a corporate redesign, Roy Disney Jr. (Walt's nephew) successfully leads the Board of Directors to replace Walt Disney's son-in-law as the CEO with Michael Eisner (Eisner, 1998, p. 146).

Redesign: Front-Back Hybrid Organization

As organizations grow and expand to the global arena, developing a redesign that fits the business processes as well as integrating other cultures becomes complex. One redesign that could benefit these types of organizations is the Front-Back Hybrid Organization design. Galbraith ascertains that this type of design provides two line organizations: one focused on the customer (the front end) while a second line focuses on products (the back end) with the objective in all cases being to achieve customer focus and responsiveness concurrent with global scale economies (Galbraith J. R., 2000, p. 238). This type of design allows organizations to develop customer-focused methodologies while allowing the organization to expand. Organizational growth places a new demand for global leaders. Black et al. identify that 85 percent of firms feel that they do not have an adequate number of global leaders and 67 percent feel that the global leaders they do have need additional skills and knowledge in order to meet the growth of the organization (Black, Morrison, & Gregersen, 1999, p. 185). The development of this type of redesign model can be used to enable companies to manage their growth expansion and grow global leaders through the development process. When the front end is based on countries, the objective is to achieve the elusive global-local combination, which results from resolving the management challenge of effectively linking the customer front with the product back (Galbraith J. R., 2000, p. 238).

Redesign Process

Organizational redesign can come from any of Nadler and Tushman's seven factors; however, it is also imperative to study organizations that have already been through the process. *The McKinsey Quarterly* completed a survey from November 9 to November 19, 2010, and received responses from 2,525 executives, of whom 1,890 had been through an organizational redesign in the past five years; this survey, which represented the full range of regions, industries, functional specialties, tenures, and company sizes, identified the top 12 reasons why their organizations underwent a redesign (Ghislanzoni, Heidari-Robinson, & Jermiin, December 2010):

1.   Responding to growth, 18 percent
2.   Cutting costs, 12 percent
3.   Moving to a best practice model, 12 percent
4.   Introducing change, 10 percent
5.   Reducing complexity, 8 percent
6.   Increasing revenues, 8 percent
7.   Fulfilling a new leader's desire to make changes, 7 percent
8.   Responding to a crisis, 7 percent
9.   Integrating previous acquisitions, 6 percent
10. Facilitating a merger, 6 percent
11. Responding to regulatory pressure, 2 percent
12. Improving risk management, 1 percent

As organizations analyze their redesign process, it is vital to understand the need for a redesign and then develop a strategic plan that will enable the success of a redesign. Many companies have successfully completed an organizational redesign and other companies have failed at redesign. Global leaders need to know the reasons for redesign success and failures. Additionally, knowledge and experience with successful redesign models like the Front-Back Hybrid model becomes even more valuable. Organizations are looking for global leaders that can effectively and productively create organizational redesigns for the future.

Chapter 5
The Common Core of
Trust & Ethics

"He who does not trust enough, Will not be trusted."
—Lao Tzu

"Educating the mind without educating the heart is no education at all."
—Aristotle

"The day soldiers stop bringing you their problems is the day you
have stopped leading them. They have lost their confidence
that you can help them or concluded that you do not care.
Either case is a failure of leadership."
—Colin Powell

Leadership is as much about who we are as what we do. This is especially
vital in building cross-culture relationships in those we lead. One of the
core ingredients to innovation is the concept of trust. Bennis identifies that
one of the core competencies of leadership is that leaders generate and
sustain trust (Bennis, 1999). Elmuti and Kathawala conclude that a lack of
trust will always lead to a leadership failure as well as a failure in strategic
alliances (Elmuti & Kathawala, 2001). Leadership style and focus will also
affect trust. Joseph and Winston determine that perceptions of servant
leadership correlated positively with leader trust and determine that
organizations perceived as servant-led exhibited higher levels of leader trust
than organizations perceived as non-servant-led (Joseph & Winston,
2005). Trust is a major factor in organizational success, and any
organization would benefit from that type of design. However, designing
an organization to instill and develop trust can be challenging.

Simons describes that perceptions parallel behavioral integrity as antecedents of trust and identifies that research on organizational behavior identifies that inconsistency between words and deeds decreases trust as well as noting how lies and distortions decrease trust, while undistorted communication reinforces trust (Simons, 1999). Distrust and ineffective communication can quickly dissolve into cynicism. According to Henry and Richard Blackaby, cynical leaders cultivate cynical followers when they are constantly criticizing others thereby modeling a critical attitude for others to follow, and it is imperative that leaders not allow themselves to be consumed by cynicism (Blackaby & Blackaby, 2001). If leaders do not earn the people's trust by living a life of integrity and being true to their values, people simply will not follow them too far.

People First

According to Sendjaya and Pekerti, trust is a mutual benefit derived from a covenantal relationship, and the leader as well as the follower has to build a trust relationship (Sendjaya & Pekerti, 2010). Pfeffer contends that putting people first is a key strategy to develop trust for successful businesses (Pfeffer, 1998, p. 17). Air Force General Hal Hornburg was well known in the military for his philosophy of leading, which was People First—Mission Always (Air Force Times, 2004). While this phrase was not original with General Hornburg, the Air Force has been promoting this emphasis on people for many years. However, this type of leadership is not unique just to the Air Force. Army Major General Reuben Jones uses this same phrase in emphasizing the need for Army leaders to balance their lives (Jones, 2010). In addition to this type of leadership spreading across US military cultures, some international coalition partners are also calling upon this type of leadership. On 31 July 2011, Air Chief Marshal Norman Anil Kumar Browne became India's 23rd Chief of the Air Staff. Air Chief Marshal Browne noted that the Indian Air Force was on the verge of transforming itself into a "potent strategic force" and unveiled his "People First Mission Always" vision for the force (*The Hindu*, 2011).

Higher trust levels build stronger ties between the leader and the follower (Sendjaya & Pekerti, 2010). Trust becomes the substance holding people together in a group or organization. Trust is a value that should transcend cultures and build strong relationships for innovative leaders. Bennis identifies four competencies of the new leader that will determine the future success for organizations (Bennis, 1999):

- The new leader understands and practices the power of appreciation. They are connoisseurs of talent and more curators than creators.
- The new leader keeps reminding people of what's important.
- The new leader and the led are intimate allies.
- The new leader generates and sustains trust.

Elements of Trust

According to Von Krogh et al., every encounter with another person establishes some degree of trust, which compensates for the lack of knowledge about that person (Von Krogh, Ichijo, & Nonaka, 2000, p. 49). Kouzes and Posner determine that trusting other people encourages their trust, but distrusting others makes them lose confidence; leaders benefit by clearly communicating trust and accessibility to their constituents (Kouzes & Posner, 1993). This type of interaction requires leaders to build upon strong levels of trust and credibility. Open lines of communication are vital links to build the levels of trust and credibility required for global leadership. Bell identifies three elements of trust making (Bell C. R., 2002):

- Trust starts with authenticity.
- Trust depends on credibility.
- Trust is enabled through communication.

Schein contends that levels of trust and openness across various boundaries are likely to be a cultural issue; therefore, it is best to start with a heterogeneous group and let the group experience the extent to which certain areas of communication are or are not inhibited by the presence of others (Schein, 1997). It is vital that leaders openly show their trust in their followers in order to allow them the freedom to release their creativity and innovation. Winston and Patterson claim that trust and credibility work together in a successful leader-follower relationship (Winston & Patterson, 2006).

Trustworthiness

The "trustworthiness" of leaders is closely tied to their ethical commitment. According to Robbins, ethics concerns the responsibility of humans to think and act in special ways in both extraordinary and ordinary circumstances (Robbins, 1996, p. 129). Bass expounds that ideologically inspired amoral theories are being produced in many business schools and management development programs across the country, which free future organizational leaders from any sense of moral responsibility for their decisions as well as encouraging, rather than inhibiting, this type of opportunistic behavior (Bass B., 2008). Simons determines that the challenge of maintaining behavioral integrity is critical for the development of trust as well as being vital for successful change efforts (Simons, 1999). This type of motivation requires leaders to build upon strong levels of trust and credibility.

Burns defines a transformational leader as one who raises the followers' level of consciousness about the importance and value of outcomes and how to effectively reach them (Burns, 1978, p. 142). Trust is required to produce these outcomes. Understanding the cultural environment is vital to leaders building relationships and earning trust. Woolfe states that if leaders have not earned the people's trust by constantly keeping their word and being true to their values, then it doesn't matter how noble or worthwhile the cause because people will not follow them too far (Woolfe, 2002). Developing relationships based upon trust will be vital to lead successful organizations in today's globally connected environment. Trust becomes a key component for leaders to build harmony in their organizations.

Harmony and Strength Based Leadership

Modern organizations can use the successful model of Tom Rath's Strength Based Leadership for their development and expansion programs. To move an organization forward, especially during hard times, the strength of harmony is a powerful enabler for organizational growth. Harmony is one of the 34 common talents in the Strength Based Leadership approach to management. For organizations to benefit from the concept of harmony, trust is vital as they look for areas of agreement and find that common ground to build upon. Rath provides four main ideas for action to build upon the strength of harmony (Rath, 2007, pp. 110-111):

- Use Harmony talents to build a network of people with differing perspectives. Rely on these people when their expertise is needed.
- When conflict is inevitable, look for points of agreement and engage others in the conversation. By increasing the number of voices in the conversation, points of agreement are more likely to emerge.
- Create interactions and forums in which people feel like their opinions are truly being heard. This will help others become more engaged in group projects and activities.
- In discussions, look for the practical side of things. Help others see this practical side. It is the starting point of agreement.

Harmony becomes the product of a trusted environment. Implementing the ideas for action of the Strength Based Leadership theme of harmony would allow modern organizations to build upon the foundation of trust and produce effective growth. Trust is also a critical component for ethical considerations in the relationship process.

Ethics seems to be one of those words that most people think they know but have trouble defining. If individuals have trouble defining ethics, then that concept is only compounded when applied to organizations. Asking 10 different people the definition of ethics will probably get 10 different responses. What if the organization has 100 people or a 1000? Then that organization may have 100 or 1000 different definitions. May states that if ethics were easy and straightforward in our organizations, there would be no need for the plethora of books and articles on the subject; ethical decision making and practice are fraught with difficulties and challenges (May, 2012).

The connection between ethics and leadership as presented by Burns establishes genuine leadership as a morally charged concept that systematically refuses to include, for example, Hitler and other despots on its list of leaders (Burns, 1978). When talking about ethics in organizations, there are two ways of approaching the subject which are the individualistic approach and the communal approach. More often than not, discussions about ethics in organizations reflect only the individualistic approach to moral responsibility and according to this approach, every person in an organization is morally responsible for his or her own behavior, which means that any efforts to change that behavior should focus on the individual (Brown, 1989).

Wren and Bedeian state that the subject of ethics deals with human moral behavior, good or bad, and has occupied the thinking of researchers from the beginning of time (Wren & Bedeian, 2009). According to Ciulla, the study of ethics generally consists of the examination of right, wrong, good, evil, virtue, duty, obligation, rights, justice, fairness, etc. in human relationships with each other and other living things (Ciulla, 2004). When dealing with organizations, an innovative leader can use the three types of leadership values regarding ethics identified by Burns (Ciulla, 2004):

- Ethical virtues—old fashioned character tests such as sobriety, chastity, abstention, kindness, altruism, and other "Ten Commandments" rules of personal conduct.
- Ethical values—honesty, integrity, trustworthiness, reliability, reciprocity, and accountability.
- Moral value—order (or security), liberty, equality, justice, and community (meaning brotherhood and sister-hood, replacing the traditional term fraternity).

When a breakdown in one of these three categories has been noted, a determination of whether the breakdown was individual or communal would benefit the leader in working with the organization to determine the type of ethical breakdown and then develop a plan to restore ethical order.

True Character is Exposed When the Pressure is On

However, as noted above, different people have different definitions of ethics and values. In his foreword to Joanne Ciulla's book ***Ethics, the Heart of Leadership***, James Burns writes (Ciulla, 2004):

Wouldn't it be lovely, in this fragmented world, if all the sets of values, and hence all the forms of leadership, could exist in happy harmony? Alas, it cannot be. The more that a community embraces ethical virtues of mutual helpfulness, the more it is likely to come into conflict with the ethical virtues of other communities. Ethical values tend to be culture-based and hence diverse. One society's honesty is another society's incivility; one society's reciprocity is another society's corruption.

Again, the complexity of the role of ethics is revealed. Like people, an organization's true character is exposed when the pressure is on. Abraham Lincoln once said that nearly all men can stand adversity, but if you want to test a man's character then give him power. The same can be said about organizations as well as people. Today, many leaders and organizations are rising to the ethical challenge.

World's Most Ethical Companies

The research-based Ethisphere® Institute is a leading international think-tank dedicated to the creation, advancement and sharing of best practices in business ethics, corporate social responsibility, anti-corruption and sustainability. Ethisphere Magazine, which publishes the globally recognized World's Most Ethical Companies Ranking™, is the quarterly publication of the Institute. For the 2012 year, a record 145 companies made the Ethisphere World's Most Ethical Companies (WME) list, which included more than three dozen industries, from aerospace to wind power, with 43 of the WME winners headquartered outside the U.S. Since the list's inception, 23 companies have made the list all six years including: Aflac, American Express, Fluor, General Electric, Milliken & Company, Patagonia, Rabobank, and Starbucks, among others.

According to the Ethisphere Institute, the World's Most Ethical Companies designation recognizes companies that truly go beyond making statements about doing business "ethically" and translate those words into action. WME honorees demonstrate real and sustained ethical leadership within their industries, putting into real business practice the Institute's credo of "Good. Smart. Business. Profit." To that end the Institute has developed a 36-page survey to determine an organization's Ethics Quotient (EQTM). While the rating system and analysis is proprietary, the survey is available online and provides a good starting point for today's organizations to develop an ethical framework. The EQTM framework consists of five core categories:

- Ethics and Compliance Program
- Reputation, Leadership and Innovation
- Governance
- Corporate Citizenship and Responsibility
- Culture of Ethics

Large organizations such as the Walt Disney Company and Microsoft have established a Director of Corporate Citizenship to operate the organization in an economically, socially, and environmentally sustainable manner, and to be transparent and accountable for their actions, behaviors, and products. While smaller organizations may not have the resources to create this type of position, the tenets of transparency and accountability can be woven throughout an organization of any size. The establishment of these tenets early in the organization will help ensure their continuity as the organization grows. This type of ethical framework goes beyond simply legal compliance and establishes a culture of ethics and a corporate citizenship responsibility requiring organizations to be responsible not just for their behavior but for their product as well.

Everyone Loves a Good Success Story

Ethical failures seem to be a common front page news story. While is there is some value in understanding the reasons for ethical failures another way of examining the role of ethics in modern organizations is to focus on ethical success stories. While it is important for organizations to know what "not to do," ethical success stories provide a measure for organizations to strive towards. Yet, success stories do not seem to make the headline news story of the day. However, constantly emphasizing ethical failures only leads to a critical or cynical outlook. Many people and organizations make good ethical decisions every day. While some in our modern day society believe that what goes on in private does not affect the outward or public image of today leaders, the current scandals of ethical failures are proving them wrong.

The University of Virginia's Darden School of Business reports in the Business Roundtable Institute for Corporate Ethics that most people know the story of Johnson and Johnson's former CEO Jim Burke and the Tylenol product recall in the 1980s in which, at a great short-term financial cost, he pulled all potentially tampered-with products off the shelves, thereby keeping the public's trust intact. As the story goes, some Tylenol had been laced with cyanide. Three people died in Chicago and seven people died altogether. Tylenol represented 18% of Johnson and Johnson's corporate income and the recall lost the corporation over 100 million dollars. According to the Business Roundtable Institute, the recall and rapid response put Johnson and Johnson in the ethics hall of fame. Many corporations have determined to focus on a successful ethic culture. However, success stories are not just limited to CEO's of Fortune 500 companies.

Ethics that Affect Millions

The works of Professor Mohammed Yunus, a Nobel Prize winner and founder of Grameen Bank as well as being known as the "father" of rural finance in Bangladesh, demonstrate how rural people and the poor can be supported to sustainably pursue their livelihood's development. Through rural finance, Bangladesh is currently a shining example in Asia where microfinance has turned the lives of hundreds of thousands and possibly millions of impoverished individuals and families from a situation of abject poverty and hopelessness to one of dignity and integrity. Former President George W. Bush stated in a speech in New York that, "America's highest economic need is higher ethical standards—enforced by strict laws and upheld by responsible business leaders." In essence, a gatekeeper role is needed.

The Gatekeeper Role

The role of a gatekeeper can be used to keep the ethics of an organization from drifting over time. The business definition of gatekeeper is a junior officer who controls the flow of information to a group of people

(BusinessDictionary.com, 2012). German researchers, Hauschildt and Schewe, conclude that in order to be successful, new organizations must establish the role of the gatekeeper who is charged with maintaining the original purpose and content of information so that it does not drift (again) or change over time (Hauschildt & Schewe, 2000).

Walt Disney and the Gatekeeper Role

The Walt Disney Company faced an ethical dilemma that the gatekeeper concept helped resolve. After the death of Walt Disney, the leadership of the Walt Disney Company developed a program called "Traditions" to impart the importance of Disney ethics, culture, heritage, values and policies as originally taught by Walt Disney (Disney Institute, 2001, p. 45). With the Traditions class firmly in place and currently taught to every employee (called cast members) on their first day at work, the visionary process of Walt Disney was restored and kept in order. The Walt Disney Company was concerned that without Walt Disney leading the company its original purpose and content of information would drift or change over time. The Traditions course provides for the role of the gatekeeper for the entire Walt Disney Company, and still promotes the Disney brand of ethics to all its cast members.

Modern day organizations would benefit from following the example of the Walt Disney Company in establishing a gatekeeper role or program to keep the organization on its original course and purpose. The Walt Disney Company instituted a gatekeeper program that allowed them to grow even larger that when Walt Disney was at the helm and allowed them to retain much of his original purpose and intent. Modern day organizations would greatly benefit by establishing the role of the gatekeeper built into their modern leadership development programs.

The Ethics Gatekeeper

Modern day organizations would benefit from following the example of the Walt Disney Company in establishing a gatekeeper role or program to keep the organization on its original course and purpose. The Walt Disney Company instituted a gatekeeper program that allowed them to grow even larger that when Walt Disney was at the helm and allowed them to retain much of his original purpose and intent. Modern day organizations would greatly benefit by establishing the role of the gatekeeper built into their modern leadership development programs.

The Walt Disney Company instituted a gatekeeper program that allowed them to grow even larger that when Walt Disney was at the helm and allowed them to retain much of his original purpose and intent. Modern day churches and organizations would greatly benefit by establishing the role of the gatekeeper as well as having the 14 value and ethical qualifications from Titus built into their modern leadership development programs and replace the secular aggressive-based value and ethical programs.

Trust & Ethical Considerations

As emerging innovative leaders of today's modern organizations, it is vital to be able to develop and acknowledge ethical success stories as well as having knowledge of ethical failures. Many business and leaders around the world are making successful ethical decisions on a daily basis. Two keys to building a successful ethical organization are to establish a culture of ethics through the gatekeeper role and a corporate citizenship responsibility inside the organization. Many organizations have developed a Director of Corporate Citizenship position to transform organizational cultures to extend beyond just behavior, but to also include their products. With many small organizations being able to access the global business economy through the use of the Internet, the ethical tenets of transparency and accountability are becoming even more important. The common core of trust and ethics may be the most complex, yet the most required core, for innovative leaders. Many times the understanding of trust and ethics requires a broader understanding of context.

Chapter 6
The Common Core of Context

"Reality is not a function of the event as an event,
but of the relationship of that event to past, and future, events."
—Robert Penn Warren, All the King's Men

"Priority is a function of context."
—Stephen R. Covey

Context is vital for all levels of communication and context is one of the major considerations for innovative leaders to communicate cross-culturally, which makes this common core of special interest to innovative leaders. Whether the subject is a new organizational policy or an overall redesign, context is a key ingredient. Many times information taken out-of-context will become problematic. Context in a cross-cultural environment is even more critical. According to Morden, it is unrealistic to take an ethnocentric and universalistic view towards the principles and practice of management as they are applied in other countries and other cultures because what works well in one country may be entirely inappropriate in another (Morden, 1999). Again, Shahin and Wright conclude that most leadership theories come from North America and may not be applicable across diverse cultures and ethnic groups, which differ from the American culture (Shahin & Wright, 2004). Morden further states that context is defined in terms of how individuals and their society seek information and knowledge (Morden, 1999). Von Krough et al. contend that the ability to create the right context is the enabling context for knowledge creation, and involves organizational structures that foster solid relationships and effective collaboration (Von Krogh, Ichijo, & Nonaka, 2000, p. 176).

Hofstede identifies that mental programs are developed early in childhood and are reinforced in schools and organizations, which leads to the development of a national culture; consequently, these values are expressed differently among people from different countries (Hofstede, 1984, p. 11). Hall distinguishes between a high-context culture and a low-context culture. People from high-context cultures obtain information from personal information networks; whereas, people from low-context cultures seek information about decisions and deals from a research base (Hall, 1976). A high-context culture places a great deal of emphasis on a person's values and position or place in society, and interactions with others, rather than on the words and formal legalistic constructs (Darling & Heller, 2011). The identification and use of cultural context takes time, experience, and practice. There are no quick solutions for understanding the context of a culture.

The Context Strategy

With the advent of globalization and with cultural interaction becoming more prevalent, developing a cross-cultural communication context strategy takes on an added dimension. However, Northouse determines that there are no established theories of cultural leadership so research becomes more of a collection of related ideas instead of a single unified theory (Northouse, 2007, p. 301). Finzel identifies communication chaos as one of the top ten mistakes that leaders make and conclude that communication strategies must have cross-cultural considerations in order to reduce chaos (Finzel, 1994, p. 113). As previously mentioned, trust becomes the outcome of effective communication across different cultures. According to Sendjaya and Pekerti, trust is a mutual benefit derived from effective cross-cultural relationships (Sendjaya & Pekerti, 2010). The establishment of relationships is a critical component of a context strategy.

However, Hofstede remarks that highlighting culture dependent differences in thinking and acting are not always welcome interventions (Hofstede, 1984, p. 8). Hall introduces the concept of context as a human behavioral influence, and he characterizes societies as being either low-context, which are typical of northern Europe, or high-context, most dramatically represented by Japan (Hall E., 1976). Context even affects language, and human speech patterns will change, depending upon who they are speaking to and the context of the communication. Marquardt and Berger settle that one of the problems of the twenty-first century workplace will involve mergers across disparate cultures, and organizations will need to respond in different ways depending on the cultural needs (Marquardt & Berger, 2000, pp. 175-176). The context of those cultural needs will necessitate the different responses.

High-Low Context

Hall states that one of the functions of culture is to provide a selective screen between man and the outside world, which designates what we choose to see as well as ignore (Hall E., 1976, p. 85). Hofstede explains that organizations are culture bound (Hofstede, 1984, p. 252). Morden determines that context is defined in terms of how individuals and their society seek information and knowledge (Morden, 1999). Again, this range of context goes from low to high. According to Schein, low-context events have universal meanings and high context events have various meanings, which can become problematic in different cultures (Schein, 1997, p. 100). People from high context cultures obtain information from personal information networks (Morden, 1999).

Before high context people make a decision, or arrange a deal, they become well informed about the facts associated with it. High context people have discussed the matter with friends, business acquaintances, and relatives as well as asking questions and listening to gossip (Morden, 1999). Hall further recognizes that messages are placed on a continuum between high-context and low context with high context having very little in the coded, explicit, transmitted part of the message; a low context message is just the opposite with the mass of the information being vested in the explicit code (Hall E., 1976, p. 91). Bass summarizes the difference between high-low context cultures when Japan, a high context culture, places a premium on listening as well as the value of agreement with criticism being more indirect through a peer because direct criticism from a leader would cause them to lose face or honor (Bass B., 2008, p. 1037).

Context and Change

According to Kotter, many organizations have a leadership deficit because the organization ignores the leadership potential in the members of that organization, thereby, not offering training or relevant role models to raise up leaders from within (Kotter, 2005). Kotter further contends that great leaders get others to move in a direction that is sensible for themselves, the business, and community (Kotter, 2005). Deming outlined three steps to get others involved in accomplishing transformative change (Deming, 1994):

- The transformative leader has a theory and understands why the transformation would bring gains to the organization as well as the people involved in the organization.
- The transformative leader feels compelled to accomplish the transformation as an obligation to the people and the organization.
- The transformative leader has a step-by-step plan and can explain it in simple terms.

For leaders to be successful in getting other cultures involved in the change process, the leader needs to convey the true meaning behind the need to change. The understanding of this meaning can help alleviate some resistance to change. According to Ulrich and Ulrich, meaning is the object of a nearly universal search, and work is a nearly universal setting for engaging in this quest; therefore, leaders are meaning makers (Ulrich & Ulrich, 2010):

- They set direction that inspires others.
- They help others participate in doing good work.
- They communicate ideas and invest in practices that shape how people think, act, and feel.

As leaders focus on getting others involved in the change process and conveying the change in clear and simple terms, resistance should decrease and readiness should increase. This process is also part of the continuous improvement process for understanding other cultures.

Innovators never stop learning, which produces a continuous improvement mindset related to change. According to Locke and Jain, the concept of continuous improvement has attracted a great deal of research and managerial interest in recent years (Locke & Jain, 1995). Covey concludes that the most powerful investment that people can ever make in their lives is their investment in continuous learning and continuous improvement (Covey, 1989, p. 289). The adoption of a continuous learning process is a vital component of a leader's growth and global leadership development. Buckler identifies that three ingredients are needed for the continuous learning process to be effective (Buckler, 1996):

- Focus to plot a course for the learning effort.
- An environment which facilitates learning.
- Techniques which enable learning to be efficient.

Context and Authenticity

Context helps knowledge and information become authentic. Authenticity can lead to the development of an authentic leadership model. According to Bennis, leadership without perspective, which leads to a point of view, is not leadership and a person cannot borrow a point of view any more than a person can borrow someone else's eyes; leadership must be authentic and original because each person is an original (Bennis W. G., 1992). From their work in Israel in 2005, Shamir and Eilam identify a four-component framework for defining authentic leadership, which includes that authentic leaders (Shamir & Eilam, 2005):

- Do not fake their leadership.
- Do not lead for status, honor, or other personal rewards.
- Are not copies but are originals.
- Are leaders whose actions are based on values and convictions.

A global leader developing a cross-cultural communication strategy should be an original and follow the framework of an authentic leader. Noted author John Mason claims that everyone is born an original and should not die a copy (Mason, 1993). In identifying what a 21st century global leader should look like, George states that today's leaders should be authentic, unique, and the genuine article as well as concluding that the only valid test of a leader is the ability to bring people together to achieve sustainable results over time (George, 2007). Applying George's conclusion to measure today's leaders may help discover who are acting and who are being authentic especially in a cross cultural environment.

Cross Cultural Context

Misapplied context in a cross cultural environment can produce a malfunctioning organizational culture. According to Fletcher and Jones, a malfunctioning organizational culture will be reflected in such indicators as poor quality of work, low levels of commitment to the organization, individuals working below capacity, high levels of absenteeism, labor turnover, poor health, alcoholism, stress, and a poor safety record (Fletcher & Jones, 1992). Madu and Jacob argue that the internet will lead to a global cross cultural transformation that will enhance global business operations by removing cultural barriers that lead to sub-optimal business operations (Madu & Jacob, 1991).

With the advent of the Internet and the global economy within many organizational frameworks, cross-cultural considerations become paramount. Many times, what is normal and acceptable in one culture is an insult in another culture. In addition to wisdom, research and communication become key aspects of building trust relationships. However, it is important to keep in mind that individuals interact with individuals, not cultures (Morrison & Conaway, 2006). According to Northouse, determining the basic dimensions and characteristics of cultures are the first step in understanding these relationships (Northouse, 2007). Canton contends that sustainable globalization will increase cross-cultural understanding by breaking down barriers among people of different nations as trade alliances grow across borders (Canton, 2006). As these barriers are removed, new communication strategies will arise.

Context and Communication Strategies

Innovators need to discover a communication strategy that is congruent to the survival of the organization by understanding the cultural context of the people. Research at the Bucharest Academy of Economic Studies states that a communication strategy is vital to the success of modern day organizations (Rodica, 2009). LaChance concludes that it's nearly impossible for an organization to perform in concert at a very high level unless all the employees are responding to a common communication strategy (LaChance, 2006). According to Kaplan and Norton an effective strategic learning process requires a shared strategic framework that communicates the strategy and enables all participants, regardless of culture, to see how their individual activities contribute to overall strategy fulfillment (Kaplan & Norton, 2001).

The Mälardalen University School of Business in Västerås, Sweden ascertains three features of developing a communication strategy to assist organizations (Johanson, Skoog, Backlund, & Almqvist, 2006):

- First, the features of connectivity, regularity and stability have the potential to assist more comprehensively in allocating attention to, and control of, the organization in relation to the defined management control and communication strategy.
- Second, these features may also enable managers to balance their attention to those items on the agenda that must be dealt with strictly on time, to meet certain operational goals.
- Third, if certain relations and connections over time are clarified, their features may assist managers in communicating and legitimizing certain activities that would be harder to legitimize, given data that are more ad hoc or structured in completely different ways.

Context in Structured and Unstructured Environments

The work by Hofstede recognizes the degree to which people prefer structure over unstructured situations. Adding to Hofstede, the second dimension of national culture has been labeled the Uncertainty Avoidance, which identifies that uncertainty about the future is a basic fact of human life through which structure is introduced in order to reduce uncertainty (Hofstede, 1984, p. 110). Bass concludes that one striking difference between organizations that differ substantially in size is how relationships become more structured and formalized in large organizations, and the Aston Model was developed to include two major organizational factors (Bass B., 2008, p. 738):

- The structuring of activities (prescribed work roles).
- The centralization of decision making (limits on distraction).

However, Galbraith cautions that structure is only one facet of organizational design, and structure can become overemphasized when it affects status or power rather than processes, rewards, and people (Galbraith J., 2002, p. 14). While structure is important to the overall direction and focus of the organization, it becomes critical that the organization does not get distracted from taking care of its people. Lee Cockerell, the former Executive Vice President of Operations at the Walt Disney World Resorts, admitted that early in his career he thought a strong brand was the most important thing in an organization. However, he soon realized that the people were the brand, and no matter how good the products or services became, an organization cannot achieve true excellence unless they can attract great people (Cockerell, 2008, pp. 85-86). Finzel concludes that one of the top ten mistakes that leaders make is putting paperwork ahead of "peoplework," and the greater the leadership role, the more important the "peoplework" (Finzel, 1994, p. 37). As emerging innovative leaders develop an understanding of the common core of context, interpersonal relationships will begin to grow and expand thereby increasing their influence and success in the organization. Context can also be used as an enabler for organizations to use foresight and forecasting.

Chapter 7
The Common Core of
Foresight & Forecasting

"The best way to predict the future is to invent it."
—Immanuel Kant

"To expect the unexpected shows a thoroughly modern intellect."
—Oscar Wilde

"It is said that the present is pregnant with the future."
—Voltaire in The Portable Voltaire

"Time Keeps on Slippin' Slippin' Slippin' into the Future."
—Steve Miller Band

A popular song from the 1970's is "Fly Like an Eagle" by the Steve Miller Band. This song went to #2 in January 1977 (Relative, 2008). Steve Miller's orientation of time was to fly into the future for a solution to present day problems. Not a bad idea. However, time orientation is not just reserved for song lyrics. According to Greenberger and Thoms, time orientation is implicit in leadership theory and explicit in leadership practice, which makes it worthy of further study (Greenberger & Thoms, 1995). Burns also identifies that developing time schemes are important in leadership theory and practice (Burns, 1978). Graham proposes that time conception is a set of basic beliefs about life that are established in a cultural context, and he described three patterns of time (Graham, 1981):

- Time as a procedural tradition.
- Time as a circular tradition.
- Time as a linear separable tradition.

Hall determines three concepts to account for cultural differences among people: time, context, and space. He further concludes that tasks can be handled through monochronicity (single tasked) or polychronicity (multi-tasked) (Hall, 1989). Research at the University of Hong Kong concludes that people approach tasks from a monochronic and/or polychronic time orientation based upon their dominant culture of upbringing (Zhang, Goonetilleke, Plocher, & Liang, 2004). Morden notes that national cultures can be derived based upon monochronicity or polychronicity, but the mixing of monochronic and polychronic cultures may give rise to constant culture clash and disagreement (Morden, 1999). As futurists are building scenarios, it is vital to understand the time orientation of the national culture and/or organization in order to view the possible futures.

Forward Thinking

For innovators, change is an ever-present reality. Therefore, the real question is what to do next with these ever-changing environments. This is where the common core of foresight and forecasting become paramount. Bass contends that leaders need to be intuitive about what comes next and try to make it happen (Bass B., 2008, p. 688). Hines concludes that forecasting should be part of the fabric of every organization, and innovative thinking should be internalized into the entire institution because it is mission critical for any organization's future (Hines, Strategic Foresight, 2006).

Can tomorrow really be seen today? The discipline of forecasting boldly declares "yes" to this question. Slaughter defines forecasting simply as forward thinking and claims that it is a mental process that is used every day: such as taking out a raincoat or an umbrella in case of rain; thinking of a convenient time to make an appointment; saving up for something; or taking precautions to avoid something (Slaughter, 1993). Taylor concludes that forecasting is a predication of what may occur in the future through the use of mathematical methods (Taylor III, 1996, p. 581). Hines considers forecasting one of the six elements of an innovative foresight framework and involves uncertainties, tools, diverging and converging approaches, and alternatives (Hines, 2006). According to Cornish, forecasting is used alongside of futuring, futurism, and future studies (Cornish, 2005, p. xi).

However, innovative forecasting is not simply about the future. Slaughter contends that the extent that we become aware of different future alternatives, we gain access to new choices in the present (Slaughter, 1993). In other words, appropriate action in the present can be determined based upon a future scenario. This could involve a scenario to avoid a future event or a scenario to create a future event. It could also be used to decide upon an action due to an impending future event. Corporate and business leaders today can incorporate these future-related scenarios into their daily decision making processes in order to produce one of their futures.

Just as the present day environment is made up of the sum total of past decisions, so the future will become the product of decisions made today. Part of the integrated definition of leadership by Winston and Patterson includes influence by humbly conveying a prophetic vision of the future in clear terms that resonates with the follower(s) beliefs and values in such a way that the follower(s) can understand and interpret the future into present-time action steps (Winston & Patterson, 2006). Successful leaders discover ways to connect their vision to the values of the organization and establish a clear vision to include the values of the followers in the organization. Patterns of activity for organizations begin to emerge as the product of connecting possible future events to current actions for the innovative leader.

Pattern Masters

Peters identifies that a future consciousness depends upon an awareness of the possibility that the future can be different from the present and the past (Peters, 1978, p. 68). This denotes the need for future leaders to be able to identify patterns. Keidel concludes that future effective leaders, managers, and organizations will comprehend their future as they become "pattern masters" being able to resolve conflicts and communicate their vision through innovative processes (Keidel, 1995, p. 139). Successful organizations of today must keep moving forward looking for new competitive advantages and becoming a "pattern master" that can lead the way. As the new leaders begin to empower workers, it is important to understand that people tend to work better cooperatively rather than competitively. According to Deming, the understanding of this profound knowledge will lead to a transformation of management which leads to the adoption of a system, and systems work best when people learn to work cooperatively rather than competitively (Deming, 1994, p. 116).

Taylor concludes that when organizations start forecasting, or predicting what may occur in the future, the most important component of the newly forecasted organization are the people who will build the organization as well as the consumers that the organization will service (Taylor III, 1996, pp. 580-581). Replacing a competitive organizational structure with a more productive cooperative environment is not just a Deming idea for North America. Research in China reveals that productivity and people maintenance values have traditionally been considered to contribute to leadership effectiveness, and cooperative rather than competitive goal interdependence mediates the relationship between these outcomes as well as determining that productivity and people-values coupled with cooperative goals provide a foundation for effective leadership (Liu, Yu, & Tjosvold, 2002). A cooperative framework paves the way for organizations to produce scenario based futures.

Scenario-Based Futures

Scenario planning is the process of developing and using a set of scenarios to explore and test decision options. Chermack notes that it is important to understand that scenarios are not strategies, but are stories of possible future environments and he identifies five phases of performance-based scenario systems (Chermack, 2011, p. 80):

- **Phase 1**- Project Preparation: Intent - Develop the purpose and define the key issue. The important stakeholder groups should be identified, individuals with a high degree of organization knowledge should be recruited, internal leaders at all levels of the organization should be identified, and the scenario team can be assembled. The scenario team manages the project.
- **Phase 2**- Scenario Exploration: Intent - Gather data using SWOT, forecasts, trend analysis, Social, Technological, Economic, Ecological, and Political (STEEP) Analysis, etc. This

phase involves data gathering both on a general level and on the specific issue under consideration. The goal of information gathering is to learn and to expand the project team's familiarity with the industry and relevant economic and social factors. A secondary goal is to gather information relevant to the specific issue or decision articulated in the project proposal. Everyone has biases, and they show up in scenario planning. A key skill is the ability to be aware of biases and head off confinement in thinking.

- **Phase 3**- Scenario Development: Intent - Develop workshops and exercises to build an innovative conversation. In scenario planning, the foundation of internal analysis is the interviews. The interviews conducted allow access to the deepest concerns of line workers, managers, and executives. Interviewing individuals or groups of people in an organization is a time-consuming and detailed process that requires commitment and skill. The next step is aimed at creating the scenario logics. The scenario logics are the general frameworks or the plots of the scenarios. Once the participants have ranked the issues by impact on the strategic agenda, and by uncertainty, the ranking space is divided roughly into a 2 x 2 matrix and named. The scenario titles are critical. Naming scenarios has to do with branding and providing titles that conjure up the concepts of the scenarios will make them memorable. Once the scenario logics have been constructed and the basic plots of four scenarios have been defined, each subgroup should task an individual to write the detailed scenario story.

- **Phase 4**- Scenario Implementation: Intent - Shows how to put the scenarios to use. The first step in putting the scenarios to use is to return to the initial purpose, problem, and question. After all, the priority of the project is to develop a variety of different ways to explore the problem and answer the question. This workshop can be informal and needs only to bring the team and decision-makers back together in a room suitable for brainstorming. The presentations should be short, involve the essence of the stories, and use colorful pictures or presentation slides to describe each scenario. The project leader then facilitates a dialogue relating back to the initial question for each scenario.

- **Phase 5**- Project Assessment - Measuring the actual outcomes relative to the expected outcomes. The goal of scenario planning is to begin a genuine conversation about the potential issues decision-makers may face, and to provide a mechanism to wonder about the future. Scenarios are not forecasts and the purpose is not to choose a scenario. Scenarios are not strategies. Scenarios provide different contexts in which to consider the risks, benefits, and implications of decisions and different ways of managing strategic options.

Futurists—Not Fortune Tellers

Modern futurism properly cultivates human foresight and ethical choice (Gary, 2008). Simply put, foresight without an ethical consideration is like trying to look at the future through glasses that only have one lens. Unfortunately, this will only produce a future with a fuzzy and grainy image. Futurists that use foresight within an ethical framework have a distinct advantage because they get to use the best of both worlds. This is not an exercise in fortune telling. It is the foundation of building a potential future grounded in the common core of ethics to produce something new and unique.

Gary further determines that more dialogue between futurists and ethicists could identify conceptual and methodological parallels in forecasting (Gary, 2008). In other words, the two working together could accomplish so much more. An ethicist is generally one whose judgment on ethics and ethical codes has come to be trusted by a specific community, and is expressed in some way that makes it possible for others to mimic or approximate that judgement. According to Peters, the future itself should take on qualities related to ethics and ethical decisions, and an ability to determine the ultimate value (or non-value) of anything that exists in the present (Peters, 1978, p. 15). Vision is much better when seen through two lenses: foresight and an ethical framework. This type of cooperative arrangement can lead to the further development of forecasting tools.

Tools

Analysts and organizational leaders can gain valuable insight and experience by having practical knowledge of the variety and uses of forecasting tools. Properly used, these tools can help analysts and leaders gain an advantage in helping organizations meet their current goals as well as building the organization for the future. Hines and Bishop said that there are many different tools or approaches an analyst can choose from for performing innovative foresight, and it is important to choose the tools well-suited to the activity at hand (Hines & Bishop, 2006, p. 98). Scenario planning is an excellent tool to choose when organizations need to look at a variety of potential futures. Chermack recognized that scenario planning is a tool for surfacing assumptions so that changes can be made in how decision makers see the environment, and it is a useful tool for changing as well as improving the quality of people's perception (Chermack, 2011, p. 3).

According to Bell and Tunnicliff, true foresight and futures development is not the product of one or two people at the top, but the product of many people's visions working together (Bell & Tunnicliff, 1996). According to Hughes and Beatty, strategy is a learning process, and effective innovative leader's use thinking, acting and influencing to make strategy a learning process (Hughes & Beatty, 2005). Tools become an effective device to enable a learning process. The UK based Advanced Institute of Management Research identifies that the SWOT (Strengths, Weaknesses, Opportunities and Threats) analysis is easily the most popular tool available, but the tools with the most users are not necessarily the ones considered by managers as the most valuable (Jarzabkowski, Giulietti, & Oliveira, 2011). Isherwood advocates that while the SWOT analysis was the most used tool, the Game Theory was the most known, but least used tool followed by Cultural Web Analysis and Value Chain Analysis; the Innovative Clock was the least known and least used tool which inferred that simpler tools are used more than complicated tools (Isherwood, 2011).

Cornish concludes that for a futures wheel, participants simply write a possible future event with a circle around it, and then expand the map with a series of possible consequences (Cornish, 2005, p. 131). The value that this procedure brings to the arena of forecasting is looking at the potential second and third order effects of decisions. Hines and Bishop report that the traditional method for identifying second and higher order implications is the futures wheel and that many organizations stop their planning at first order implications thereby failing to get potentially important downstream implications (Hines & Bishop, 2006, p. 146). The futures wheel can increase the awareness of the organization's leaders to the possible implications of their decisions. Watson determines that the future will not be a singular experience nor is it a foregone conclusion and people of the same age, with the same job, living on the same street will experience the future in different ways, which will be heavily influenced by local as well as highly personal events (Watson, 2012, p. 296).

These types of "life experiences" are produced by second and third effects to decision points made in the past. According to Sanders, visual thinking is the key to innovative thinking, and innovative thinking has two major components: insight about the present and foresight about the future (Sanders T. I., 1998). Innovative leaders that can look into the possible futures of an organization can quickly become invaluable to leading the growth and expansion of that organization.

Chapter 8
The Common Core of
Rest & Renewal

"Rest is not idleness, and to lie sometimes on the
grass under the trees on a summer's day, listening to
the murmur of water, or watching the clouds float
across the sky, is by no means a waste of time"
—John Lubbock
English Biologist and Politician, 1834-1913

"Every person needs to take one day away. A day in which one consciously
separates the past from the future. Jobs, family, employers, and friends can
exist one day without any one of us, and if our egos permit us to confess,
they could exist eternally in our absence. Each person deserves a day away
in which no problems are confronted, no solutions searched for. Each of us
needs to withdraw from the cares which will not withdraw from us."
—Maya Angelou, *Wouldn't Take Nothing for My Journey Now*

Rest and renewal are often-forgotten topics of leadership (Vanderpyl,
2012). Today's leaders are pressed on every side to produce more with less,
and work until the project is finished. Bass concludes that U.S. employees
work longer hours than their European counterparts in order to maintain a
higher output of products which is a major cause of stress (Bass B., 2008,
p. 813). According to Maslach and Leiter, organizations are enhancing
productivity through the use of sophisticated technology to get more done
with fewer people (Maslach & Leiter, 1997, p. 5).

Many times, leaders are revered for their work ethic, but rarely for their
"rest ethic" (Vanderpyl, 2012). According to Maslach and Leiter, work

overload is a leading cause of burnout, and burnout greatly affects the bottom line of any organization (Maslach & Leiter, 1997, p. 65). Covey contends that success in life involves caring for the physical dimension in getting sufficient rest and relaxation (Covey, 1989, p. 289). O'Neil states that no success is worth the high toll it can take on a person's health, relationships, and peace of mind (O'Neil, 1993, p. 84). Burn out can become the product of this high toll.

Burn Out

Burn out is the likely product of over extending commitments in life. However, cultural influences can provide strength during a time of extended commitments for a short period of time. Nadler and Tushman determine that culture is centered in the ideologies, political alliances, collective self-images, webs of influence, career expectations, and patterns of behavior in people (Nadler & Tushman, 1997, p. 194). Research at the University of the South Pacific in Fiji identify that culture influences our thinking and consequently our behaviors, and social justice is about recognizing our values, philosophies, processes, and structures in our education system and that theorizing social justice should be founded on our knowledge systems that are embedded in our cultures (Fua, 2007). Hofstede defines culture as the programming of the mind that differentiates one group from another group (Hofstede, 2001). According to Bass, cultures clearly differ in what are seen as important traits of character (Bass B., 2008, p. 221). It is these components of culture and family that provides the strengths needed to accomplish individual purpose. These components can also provide strength during times of burnout. However, Maslach and Leiter conclude that when people continually bring burnout home, their exhaustion and negative feelings begin to affect relationships with family and friends (Maslach & Leiter, 1997, p. 19). This point of exhaustion leads some to search for rest and renewal.

When to Renew

While renewal comes in different forms for different people, there are some common factors or signs that can indicate when a person needs a period of renewal. According to O'Neil, one major factor is when a people come home from work physically, but psychologically remain imprisoned by the roles they have created for themselves at work (O'Neil, 1993, p. 24). Multiple signs such as working as much from home after getting home, or constantly having to answer the phone for work related calls may be indicators. People may spend years climbing the ladder of success only to reach the top and find that it is leaning against the wrong wall (Parsons, 2007, p. 48). It is vital for leaders to be able to pause and monitor the events and places around them in order to ensure that they are climbing the right wall.

Willard concludes that the inability to find adequate answers in life leaves people rudderless in the flood of events, and people are at the mercy of whatever ideas as well as forces that come to bear upon them (Willard, 2002, p. 16). Fatigue can also become the product of a flood of events and is another indicator of when rest and renewal is needed. Wuellner contends that fatigue is deep and pervasive (Wuellner, 1998, p. 109). Bass determines that fatigue and stress can produce faulty decision making, absenteeism, irritability at work, and a confused appearance (Bass, 2008, p. 812). The ability to identify when a person needs to pause, rest, and renew is paramount to not being swept away in the flood of these life events. Renewal is considered by many to be the hidden key for a successful life. No one really starts out in life to fail. However, stress and burnout are becoming more commonplace today. At some point in the life of every individual and organization, the need for renewal becomes vital and even nature, itself, proclaims the need for periodic renewal to succeed (O'Neil, 1993, p. 122).

Guidelines for rest may be unique to given situations, but the requirement for rest and renewal should be emphasized across the organization. Vanderpyl produced the following suggestions to form a baseline policy for rest and renewal (Vanderpyl, 2012):

- Create mandatory "no smart-phone" times with teams. Leaders must set this example themselves and enforce it with their team. For example, a leader could mandate no checking or sending e-mails between midnight and 6 a.m. and on Sundays.
- Ensure and enforce a mandatory "no contact" practice between

employees and the office while they are on vacation. This would need to prevent employees from contacting the office for any reason, and prevent employees still working from contacting the vacationing employee while he or she is away. Again, leaders must set a firm example in their own actions.

- Find ways to creatively praise employees who ask for time off for special family events, rather than praising those who sacrifice family events for the sake of work projects. Occasional projects may interfere with family time, but that should be known as an exception, not the norm.

- Find reasons, when possible, to send employees home early at random times with the mandate to relax at home. Many times, sport coaches rest their star players in games at the end of the season when that game does not actually matter. Work tends to be cyclical throughout the year, with busy and less-busy times. Leaders could use those less-busy times to rest their employees in anticipation of upcoming busy times.

Stress Management

Sporadic patterns of rest and renewal can easily increase the amount of stress a leader feels. Stress management becomes a primary concern for these leaders. Maslach and Leiter conclude that the majority of the stress management techniques are mistakenly designed to change the individual rather than the situation (Maslach & Leiter, 1997, p. 70). McCall and Hollenbeck describe that stable personal life situations are essential in maintaining stress-resistant personal arrangements, usually family, that supports a commitment to work and dealing with complexity (McCall Jr. & Hollenbeck, 2002, p. 36). Stress management solutions are not necessarily easy or "quick win" solutions for an organization. According to Fletcher and Jones, a malfunctioning organizational culture will be reflected in such indicators as poor quality of work, low levels of commitment to the organization, individuals working below capacity, high levels of absenteeism, labor turnover, poor health, alcoholism, stress, and a poor safety record (Fletcher & Jones, 1992).

Bass cautions that a hasty change can produce a high level of stress and tension (Bass B. , 2008). Quick and easy solutions are not always enduring and productive solutions. Balance provides a much better approach to stress management. Covey calls this the Production/Production Capability Balance (Covey, 1989):

> Production is referred to as a useful product (either tangible or intangible) that is being produced. Production Capacity is the process or method in which that product is being produced. The product is usually a result that is either produced continually or on a regular basis thereby introducing the necessity of keeping P (Production) and PC (Production Capacity) in balance. True effectiveness is a function of two things: what is produced and the producing asset or capacity to produce.

According to Covey, when organizations fail to respect this balance, they decrease in organizational effectiveness, which can lead to stress, and he provides the following example from Aesop's fable of the goose that laid the golden eggs for his point (Covey, 1989):

> A man had the good fortune to possess a goose that laid a golden egg every day. Lucky though the man was, he soon began to think he was not getting rich fast enough, and, imagining the bird must be made of gold inside, he decided to kill it to secure the entire store of precious metal at once. But when he cut it open he found it was just like any other goose. Thus, he neither got rich all at once, as he had hoped, nor enjoyed any longer the daily addition to his wealth.

The point Covey makes with this story is that people must balance the production capability, or "PC" (in this case, the goose), to get the product, or the "P" (that is, the golden eggs). Just as the man in the fable didn't take care of his goose, leaders need to be careful not to ignore their health, family, relaxation, and religious activities by spending too much time and activity on work (Kaniss, 2006). Balancing production capability, product, and time away from work will help leaders balance stress management with life events. Block contends that the current mindset of modern society is a one-minute culture in which speed is God and time is the devil; the need for speed becomes an obstacle for real change and may only increase stress

(Block, 2001). This type of drive produces stressful situations in the life of the leader and the organization. At this point, stress management of the organization becomes paramount instead of the stress managements solutions of the individual.

It is vital when climbing the ladder of success to pause, rest, and renew in order to ensure that the ladder is up against the correct wall. There is little value in getting to the top of the ladder only to find that it is leaning against the wrong wall. The stress and burn-out of the long hours will only lead to a life of loneliness and empty desires. Rest and renewal are critical competencies for innovative leaders to successfully thrive in today's environment. Faulty decision making and lack of productivity due to stress and burn-out will not lead to long successful careers. Rest and renewal need to be considered on a regular basis to ensure a proper balance in life's goals. Stop and plan today for a time of rest and renewal. The world and your workplace will be better off with this renewal.

Chapter 9
The Common Core of Leadership Succession

"Life is a succession of lessons which must
be lived to be understood."
—Helen Keller

"Nature gives to every time and season some beauties
of its own; and from morning to night, as from the cradle
to the grave, it is but a succession of changes so gentle
and easy that we can scarcely mark their progress."
—Charles Dickens

"One of the things we often miss in succession planning
is that it should be gradual and thoughtful, with
lots of sharing of information, and knowledge with
perspective, so that it's almost a non-event when it happens."
—Anne M. Mulcahy, Former Xerox CEO

The common core of leadership succession may be one of the most overlooked competencies until leaders near the end of their tenure. However, successful leadership succession actually begins on day one. Finzel states that one of the top mistakes that leaders make is having success with a successor, and he concludes that leaders need to plan their departure on the day they begin (Finzel, 1994, p. 157). Therefore, innovative leaders need to develop a strategy for leadership succession. Bass explains that traditional succession strategies promote from within when potential successors are assessed, developed, and coached for numerous leadership positions with opportunities for internal and external training

(Bass B., 2008, p. 886). Rothwell contends that one of the keys to effective succession planning is communicating upward and laterally concerning management of the organization (Rothwell, 2005, p. 19). The future of many good organizations will be realized as leaders work hand-in-hand with others in the organization to produce a healthy climate of cooperation in succession planning. This is especially true for organizations that have transformational and/or charismatic leaders.

Transformation and Charismatic Leaders

The study of transformational and charismatic leadership is relatively recent, but the research has been steadily growing. Burns first introduced the transforming leader in 1978 when he concluded that transforming leadership was best built upon a relationship of mutual stimulation and elevation that converts followers into leaders and leaders into moral agents (Burns, 1978). While charismatic leadership can be regarded as part of transformational leadership, some research indicates that the undesirable consequences at the societal level of charismatic leadership include totalitarian aspects as well as truth manipulation practiced by some charismatic leaders (Aaltio-Marjosola & Takala, 2000).

Khurana issues a caution concerning charismatic-only leaders when he states that the charismatic succession process implies that a single individual deserves vastly more attention and rewards than anyone else in the organization, and ignores the reality that organizational performance is driven by more than one person (Khurana, 2002, p. 197). Bass relates the dynamics of the charismatic leader-follower relationship and concludes that charismatic leaders often use themselves as examples for their subordinates to follow (Bass B., 2008, p. 590). Khurana concludes that many organizations focus on the charisma of the organizational leader and seriously underestimate the risk of outside succession (Khurana, 2002, p. 188). Northouse identifies four specific types of charismatic behavior (Northouse, 2007, pp. 178-179):

- They are strong role models for the beliefs and values they want their followers to adopt.
- They appear competent to followers.

- They articulate ideological goals that have moral overtones.
- They communicate high expectations for followers and they exhibit confidence in their followers' abilities to meet these expectations.

Bass posits that charismatics can foster antisocial behavior, and personalized charismatic leaders can be dominant, self-interested, and authoritarian (Bass B., 2008, p. 578). While charismatic and transformational leadership styles are similar, there are some differences; especially when measured against the servant leadership style. According to Stone, Russell, and Patterson, transformational leaders direct their focus toward the organization, so their behavior builds follower commitment toward organizational objectives, while servant leaders focus on their followers, and the achievement of organizational objectives is a subordinate outcome (Stone, Russell, & Patterson, 2004). Kotter concludes that many organizations have a leadership deficit because the organization ignores the leadership potential in the members of that organization, thereby, not offering training or relevant role models to raise up leaders from within (Kotter, 2005). Deming outlines three steps to get others involved in accomplishing transformative change (Deming, 1994):

- The transformative leader has a theory and understands why the transformation would bring gains to the organization as well as to the people involved in the organization.
- The transformative leader feels compelled to accomplish the transformation as an obligation to the people and the organization.
- The transformative leader has a step-by-step plan and can explain it in simple terms.

A transformational leader can make the organization more successful by valuing its human capital. Northouse determines that the effect of organizational change through transformational leaders is the ability of the transformational leader to be a role model, create a vision, and empower followers to facilitate ownership of the process (Northouse, 2007).

Bell indicates that the challenge for all learning facilitators is the actual transfer of learning (Bell C. R., 2002, p. 133). This is true for establishing leadership succession principles and traits. Organizations of today can use choose to follow this pattern. It is vital for leaders of today to creatively identify the unique strengths of their organization and start the leadership succession process as soon as possible. Rothwell identifies that one of the ten key trends on succession planning and management is the importance of values and competencies (Rothwell, 2005, p. 42). Therefore, the innovative leaders' response to succession planning is to identify the next generation of leaders and develop them based upon their unique strengths to continue the work.

Chapter 10
The Common Core of
Mentoring & Discipleship

"Tell me and I forget, teach me and I may remember,
involve me and I learn."
—Benjamin Franklin

"The pen is mightier than the sword."
—Edward Bulwer-Lytton

Words are powerful. In 1839, Edward Bulwer-Lytton coins the phrase for a play which says, "The pen is mightier than the sword." However, the thought was not unique to him. As early as 406 BC, the Greek poet Euripides said, "The tongue is mightier than the blade." Two words that contain infinite power for innovative leaders are discipling and mentoring.

Words of Action and Change

Mentoring and discipling are two words of action and change. Their reach is beyond time and space. However, these words are not interchangeable and will produce different results. According to Bell, mentoring focuses on helping others learn (Bell C. R., 2002, p. 5). Bekker extends that concept to conclude that mentoring is follower-centric (Leadership Talks, 2007). Mentoring is based upon relationship and focuses on leaders working with followers to be all that they can be (Puryear, 2002, p. 189). The mentor's goal is to help followers accomplish the followers' plans.

Discipling produces a different outcome. Winston defines discipling as leader-centric where a person is learning from the leader and wants to be like the leader (Leadership Talks, 2007). Under this banner, followers may give up their own personal plan to take on the vision or purpose of the leader. Discipling is leader-centric and focuses on the followers becoming like the leader in some area of their life. As emerging innovative leaders, it takes wisdom to be able to determine which role to use in developing followers. Both roles are valuable, but produce different outcomes.

Discipling Transcends Time and Space

Bekker recognizes four important aspects of discipleship (Leadership Talks, 2007):

- Followers must desire to learn and be like the master or leader.
- Followers must say no to their own plans and die to self.
- Followers take up the vision of the leader.
- Followers take up the quest of the leader.

Winston adds that discipling does not need to be a face-to-face encounter (Leadership Talks, 2007). He describes a self-study process that he went through with W. Edwards Deming and found that he wanted to be like him in some areas. Even though he had never met Deming, he found himself being "discipled" by Deming's work.

Discipling produces a different outcome. Again, discipling is leader-centric where a person is learning from the leader (or master) and wants to be like the leader. Therefore, followers give up their plans in order to take on the vision or purpose of the leader.

According to Bekker, a disciple is like an apprentice in modern times (Leadership Talks, 2007). Again, both roles are valuable, but produce different outcomes. Mentoring produces a diverse group of people each accomplishing their own vision and purpose; discipling produces a group which looks, speaks, and acts the same as they pursue a common vision.

Mentoring: Face-to-Face Encounters

On the other hand, mentoring requires more of a face-to-face encounter. Since mentoring relies upon relationship, there is an implication of time being spent with the person being mentored. General Dwight Eisenhower was once asked by Edgar Puryear how a person can be developed as a decision maker. The General replied that the key was to be around people who made decisions and rely on them as mentors (Puryear, 2002, p. 188). Hendricks claims that the mentoring relationship is about becoming a marked man and focuses on helping people (Hendricks & Hendricks, 1995, p. 13). Leaders are to mark and make a significant impact on their followers. Mentoring requires that one-on-one time to be effective. However, discipling can be accomplished through the study of the documents left behind. Mentoring and discipling are important measures or competencies to build innovative leaders and teams.

Teamwork

Teamwork is a key enabler for organizations. Bass states that in designing an organization a balance needs to be struck among three variables: centralized control, decentralized autonomy, and cooperative teamwork; control and cooperation need to be balanced between consistency and flexibility (Bass B., 2008, p. 738). Bossidy identifies that an essential behavior for leaders is to know your people and know your business in order to successfully change organizational plans and structures (Bossidy & Charan, 2002). Cooperative teamwork helps to produce an environment where people know each other and work together to make a difference. Deming states that the idea that competition is a necessary way of life needs to be discarded and replaced with the idea of cooperation because, over time, competition squeezes out the innate intrinsic motivation, self-esteem, and dignity of an individual and then replaces it with fear, self-defense, and extrinsic motivation (Deming, 1994).

Bennis claims that a shrinking world in which technological and political complexity increase at an accelerating rate offers fewer arenas in which individual action and top-down leadership suffices (Bennis, 2000). The future of many good organizations will be realized as leaders work hand-in-hand with others in the organization to produce a healthy climate of cooperation. Replacing a competitive organizational structure with a more productive cooperative environment is not just a Bennis and Deming idea for North America. As previously mentioned, research in China contends that productivity and people maintenance values have traditionally been considered to contribute to leadership effectiveness and cooperative rather than competitive goal interdependence mediates the relationship between these values and outcomes (Liu, Yu, & Tjosvold, 2002). Cooperative teamwork build unity in an organization.

Team Building and the Power of Unity

Team building and the power of unity are amazing forces in an organization. Tushman and O'Reilly state that the implementation of change is enhanced when groups work together (Tushman & O'Reilly, 2002, p. 116). This power of unity works for modern day organizations as well. When former Disney CEO Michael Eisner realized that his top executives would work better if they were developed as a team, he instituted a program called Disney Dimensions for his top team, which he dubbed his synergy boot camp (Woolfe, 2002, p. 140). For eight days, these executives experienced every aspect of the theme park where they made the beds in the hotels, worked in the kitchen, cleaned bathrooms, cut hedges, checked out guests, and soothed tired children. The executives keep up this routine from 7:00 A.M. to 11:00 P.M. for over a week and this experience forged them into a team that willingly, even enthusiastically, sacrificed individual ego for the unity and goals of the group (Eisner, 1998, p. 237).

Mentoring for Today's Leaders

Mentoring relationships are methods directed toward change, and mentoring is a relationship oriented process. Bell defines mentoring as a learning process whereby the mentor teaches or guides the less learned (Bell C. R., 2002, p. 3). The focus is on the follower becoming more competent by virtue of learning and practicing. According to Zachary, many employees often seek guidance from a senior person in their organization, but are deeply disappointed with the lack of mentoring relationships; such disappointments often lead to staff turnover (Zachary, 2005). To establish a successful mentoring program that can be used globally, organizations can look at producing a model or compatible program which can be used. Bell introduces the SAGE model for mentoring (Surrendering, Accepting, Gifting, and Extending) (Bell C. R., 2002, p. 14):

- *Surrendering (S)* is all about actions that make mentoring a power-free experience. We have learned that power, authority, and command—or at least the protégé's perception of these traits in the mentor—can doom the mentoring experience to a perfunctory dialogue... sans risks, sans spirit, and sans discovery.

- *Accepting (A)* in the SAGE model focuses on the value of a safe, nontoxic relationship. When the protégé believes he or she is in a relationship that is not dangerous, growth-producing risk and experimentation are more likely to occur. The perception or prediction of danger is related not to physical harm but rather to the emotional damage caused by rebuke, judgment, or criticism—all of which yield a loss of protégé self-esteem in front of an important person. Why is this important? Without risk there is no learning; without experimentation there is no progress.

- *Gifting (G)* is positioned as the main event in mentoring. Many mentors start their mentoring relationships with a gift of advice, feedback, or focus. However, when offered as the first step in the relationship, the act of bestowing such gifts risks their being at best undervalued, at worst ignored, resisted, or rejected. If Gifting follows Surrendering and Accepting, it is more likely to be experienced by the protégé as a sincere gesture and a valued contribution worthy of attention, tryout, and effort.

- *Extending (E)* in the SAGE is about the creation and nurturance of the protégé as a self-directed learner. It is also about ways to extend the learning of the protégé beyond his or her relationship with the mentor. Essentially, it is shepherding the transfer of learning.

Gregson categorizes the various aspects of starting a mentoring culture to include deciding on objectives as well as selection, training, and matching mentors to certain junior staff (Gregson, 1994). Mentoring programs that focus upon relationship building should provide a good cross-cultural solution. However, this requires the mentor to have regular face-to-face sessions with the follower. The mentoring process needs time for the relationship to develop and the process to work through a multitude of issues. Major General (retired) William Cohen defines mentoring as taking care of your people, which he calls the Sixth Universal Law of Leadership (Cohen W. A., 1998).

Again, Bell indicates that the challenge for all learning facilitators is the actual transfer of learning (Bell C. R., 2002, p. 133). This is true for mentoring as well as establishing a common core of competencies for emerging innovative leaders. It is vital for leaders to start the mentoring or discipling process as soon as possible in order to spend as much time as needed and complete the tasks at hand of working with, as well as understanding, people.

Chapter 11
The Common Core of
Understanding People

"Those who know, do. Those that understand, teach."
—Aristotle

While ethics may be the most complex common core for innovative leaders, understanding people could be the most difficult. Understanding people may be accomplished through studying human behavior – preferences, avoidances, motivations, responses, etc. Carbonell states that the study of personalities is called the study of human behavior (Carbonell, 1993). Bass correlates personalities into two overall leadership styles: task-oriented and relations-oriented (Bass B., 2008). Hersey and Blanchard contend that structure (task) and consideration (relationships) are the two most important leadership dimensions in describing how a leader performs and concludes that high ratings on both dimensions characterize effective or desirable leadership (Hersey & Blanchard, 1969).

Bennis claims that the new reality is that intellectual capital, brain power, know-how, and human imagination has supplanted monetary capital as the critical success factor and leaders will have to learn an entirely new set of skills that are not understood, not taught in our business schools, and, for all of those reasons, rarely practiced (Bennis, 1999). Task-oriented and relations-oriented leadership styles are part of this reality that Bennis references. As innovative leaders begin to look inward for ways to move and motivate people rather than looking outward for new programs or the latest fads, the development, expansion, and maturity of their leadership styles come into focus. According to Hersey and Blanchard, depending on the maturity of subordinates, a manager should be task-oriented and tell or sell subordinates regarding what to do; or a manager should be relations-oriented and participate with subordinates in joint decision making; or the decisions should be delegated to them (Hersey & Blanchard, 1969).

Task Oriented or Relations Oriented

Bass claims that powerful autocratic or task-oriented leaders throughout history have often been praised for their ability to develop reliable and devoted followers and to act as the principal authority figures in establishing and maintaining order (Bass B., 2008, p. 440). A common perception is that leaders who are more task-oriented will achieve higher levels of task accomplishment. However, no differences were found in performance when leaders evidenced a more relationship-oriented style of leadership (Tabernero, Chambel, Curral, & Arana, 2009). Which leadership style works best may depend on the leader and the followers. However, as Plato observed, there may be no time for a democratic vote on a ship in a storm. Bass further determines that most executives who make it to the top of their organizations are task-oriented, but many are also inclined to be concerned with their relationships (Bass B., 2008, p. 497). He also contends that leaders have to be strong and decisive, yet sensitive to the needs of the followers. Even though only two leadership styles seem to be prevalent in research, there are many different expressions of these styles.

The relations-oriented style may be active or passive. Where an active relations style is expressive, demonstrative, inspirational, influential, and impressive towards a group, the passive expression becomes more focused on individual people and prefers to work one-on-one or in small groups. Many times, the more active personalities will take the credit for much of the work completed by people with a passive or reserved style. However, the passive style would strongly prefer NOT to be in the limelight or get any of the attention. Their quiet nature leads them to be more thoughtful and intuitive of people. The passive or reserved relations-oriented leader prefers a steady pace, security, and does not like sudden change. These leaders are calm, relaxed, patient, possessive, predictable, deliberate, stable, consistent, and tend to be unemotional and poker-faced. These leaders are not strong task-oriented people. Their strength is in looking out for others.

They are much more interested in the general welfare of the people in the group rather than actually getting the work done.

The task-oriented leadership style can also be active or passive (reserved). The active style is more demanding, dominating, and decisive. However, the passive expression of task-oriented leaders becomes more cautious, calculating, compliant to their own standards, and prefers a checklist of items to be accomplished. The active leader may have to help these people with the list, but once it has been developed they will work tirelessly and efficiently in completing the list.

One of the roles in the mentoring or discipling process is to develop a team to work together in order to accomplish a goal or task. It is the function of the leader to move that group from the unknown parts of the task to the known and accomplished parts. Effective leaders will select the best team members. This is where the initial challenge begins. The most difficult part of accomplishing a task or goal is not the actual work involved, nor is it merely the identification of the task or goal. The most difficult part is the one that is often overlooked—selecting the team.

Too many times, the membership of a team is simply who is present at the time. Many times, leaders will simply survey the room, pick the people that they like (or are like them) and form the team, which is then sent out to accomplish working together to develop a solution or accomplish a task. However, a reliable system is a better alternative to the best guess method. Just as team has four letters, the key to putting together a successful team has four letters: DISC. The DISC form of understanding people is not a new concept; it has been around for many years.

DISC Model

As early as 400 BC, Hippocrates notes that four basic elements of nature could be identified as humors and ties them to personal behavioral patterns in people (LaHaye, 1983). Several hundred years later around 190 AD, a Greek physician named Galenus of Pergamum, who is better known as Galen, recognizes four common temperaments. Galen names these four temperaments or personality patterns as choleric, sanguine, phlegmatic, and melancholy (Littauer & Littauer, 2006). Other studies map four types of animals, four types of strategies, four types of attitudes, four types of characters, four types of world views—even four types of thinking. Most studies always find four types of behavioral patterns. The DISC model of personality behavior builds upon these. The DISC model is the acronym for (Carbonell, 1993):

- Dominance – relating to control, power and assertiveness.
- Influence – relating to social situations and communication.
- Steadiness – relating to patience, persistence, and thoughtfulness.
- Conscientiousness – relating to structure and organization.

The original DISC Assessment Model was developed by John Geier and was based on the 1928 work of psychologist William Moulton Marston (Carbonell, 1993). DISC is the four quadrant behavioral model developed to examine the patterns of behavior for understanding people in specific situations. Most people will express or blend two of the four styles in varying degrees. Although all four contribute to the overall final expression, these blends start with the primary (or stronger) type, followed by the secondary (or lesser) type (Parsons, 2012).

These four areas of the DISC model closely correspond to Hippocrates original description of humors. Additionally, they can be grouped in a grid with "D" and "I" sharing the top row and representing outgoing or extroverted aspects of a person's behavior, while the "C" and "S" represent a passive or introverted aspect. "D" and "C" represent task-focused aspects, and "I" and "S" represent social aspects. A simple matrix can better explain (Carbonell, 1993):

The system identifying dimensions of observable behavior has become known as the universal language of behavior. DISC research has found that characteristics of behavior can be grouped into these four major behavioral styles or expressions, and they tend to exhibit specific characteristics common to that particular style. All individuals will operate or express all four types of patterns, but what differs from one to another is the extent of each (Parsons, 2012).

DOMINANT		INSPIRING
Driving	Active/Outgoing	Interesting
Doer		Interactive

Task-oriented ← **D I C S** → People-oriented

CAUTIOUS		SUPPORTIVE
Competent	Reflective/Passive/	Steady
Careful	Reserved	Stable

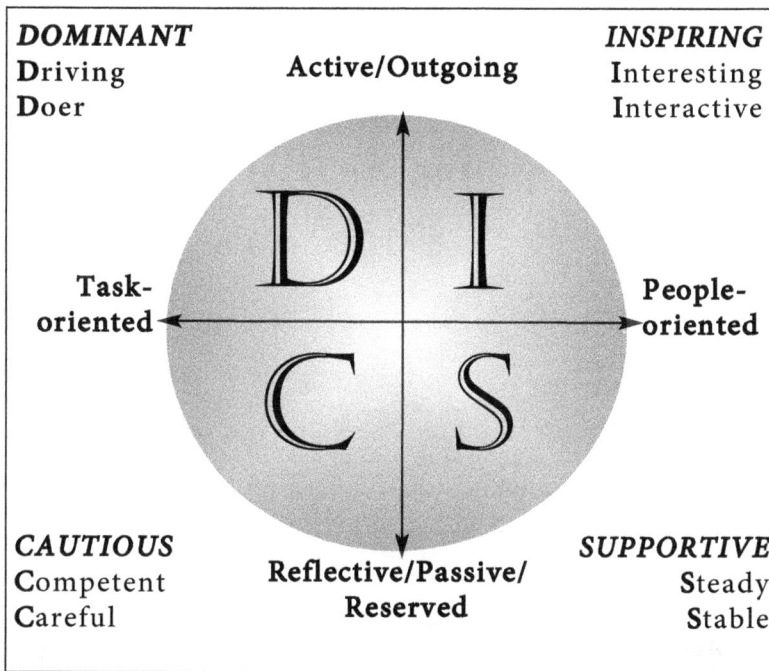

DISC Model graph by Carbonell

Understanding the differences between these blends makes it possible to integrate individual team members with less troubleshooting. In a typical team, there are varying degrees of compatibility, not just toward tasks, but interpersonal relationships as well. However, when they are identified, energy can be spent on refining the results. Each of these types adds its own unique value to the team, general characteristics, ideal environment, what the individual is motivated by, and value to the team. To create the most effective team is to bring together all four elements of the DISC model. Each member will have a purpose and role on the team. Always strengthen your strengths and staff your weaknesses in the team development process (Parsons, 2012). Team building begins with adding the missing personality pieces.

DISC Types: D—Direct and Demanding

The "D" type person is closely related to the Type "A" personality. This personality can be very demanding, direct, and dominating. No challenge is

D

DOMINANT, DIRECT, DEMANDING, DOING & DRIVING

ACTIVE & TASK-ORIENTED

Active/Outgoing

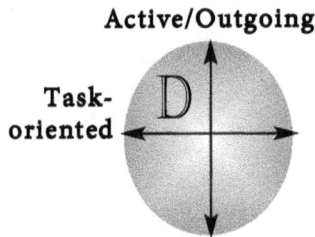

Task-oriented D

Greatest Strength:
> Getting a task started

Greatest Fear:
> Being embarrassed

Greatest Challenges:
> Not finishing tasks
> Submitting to authority

Need to focus on:
> The value of others
> Finishing Tasks

too big and no obstacle is too hard to overcome. Persistence and determination become common characteristics. They love a challenge and love to challenge anything and everything. For this person, the status quo only exists to be changed and re-created. People who are high in their intensity of the "D" style are active in dealing with problems and challenges, while low "D's" are people who want to do more research before committing to a decision. High "D" people are described as demanding, forceful, egocentric, strong-willed, driving, determined, ambitious, aggressive, and pioneering.

In contrast to that, people who score more as a low "D" are described as those who are conservative, low-key, cooperative, calculating, undemanding, cautious, mild, agreeable, modest, and peaceful. High "D" personalities are people that change the world around them. They make great entrepreneurs as well as world class criminals. Statements such as, "My way or the highway" are commonplace. They are movers and doers. This personality is active towards tasks; however, they don't specialize in task completion. These people will have ten ongoing tasks and will be ready to take on more. Their greatest challenge is to focus on completing a task prior to starting a new one. They are goal-oriented, but will seldom take the time to write things down. All of their plans exist in their head, not on paper. They like to "shoot from the hip" and ask questions later. They will ask for forgiveness after the fact, rather than permission up-front.

Hand these people a task and they will quickly start the process. While they are not always seen as a team player, their value to the team is to get things started and moving; they help overcome inertia. This personality does not like to work in a closely supervised environment as this will quench their ideas and actions. A "D" type personality does not have, use, or think they need any social interaction skills. For them, it is all about the tasks—not the people. They have a tendency to be explosive and afterwards take you to the best restaurant in town for lunch as if nothing ever happened. They are always moving forward. What happened in the past is behind them. Their mind is already on the future.

A "D" leader must realize that people are important, and tasks need to be completed. This type of person enjoys starting tasks and will easily have many different projects going at once. Finishing projects or tasks is not one of their strong points. It is important to remember to focus on one task at a time and bring it to completion.

"D's" must learn to come under authority and work within the established guidelines. They don't play well with others, and they do not like their decisions challenged. However, given the proper information and options, they will change a decision at a moment's notice. They believe that a decision is made to be changed, and the only purpose for a plan is to have something to change! They are spontaneous and work well under pressure. Actually, pressure simply becomes a catalyst to start more tasks. Many times, they become the "go-to" person because of their ability to get things started. This personality is hard-driving and hard charging. They will often run over people to get the task started and to keep the task moving forward.

Their greatest strength is also their greatest weakness. The strength of persistence and determination will cause a "D" personality to look, and perhaps become, arrogant and self-willed. To guide a "D" personality towards maturity requires tempering persistence with discipline and to match determination with empathy. It is important for "D's" to be able to sincerely show care and compassion when working with people. It is vital to remember that people are NOT tools to use in completing a task, but those people are valuable and important.

DISC Types: I—Inspiring and Influential

In addition to the "D," the "I" personality is also very active. Whereas the "D" person is active toward tasks, this personality is active toward people. They are charismatic and can be charming and may come across as manipulating other people to get their way. While there is no "I" in team, there is definitely the word, "me", and that is the basis for the "I" personality. It's all about "me." Anyone is welcome to come along on the journey, but just remember who the journey is about. The "I" personality is the life of the party. This person will talk to anyone at the "drop of a hat"

I

INSPIRING, INFLUENTIAL, INTERESTING & INTERACTIVE

ACTIVE & PEOPLE-ORIENTED

Active/Outgoing

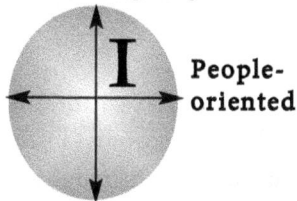

People-oriented

Greatest Strengths:
> Bring a group together
> Flexibility & spontaneity

Greatest Fear:
> Being overlooked

Greatest Challenge:
> Sharing the spotlight with others

Need to focus on:
> Organization
> Time management
> Listening

and will even drop the hat just to be able to talk. The "I" personality never meets a stranger and you will leave the conversation thinking that you are their new best friend.

The classic example of this person is the kid in class who raises their hand to answer a question, but when called on they have no idea of what the question even was. This is the untainted "I" personality. Their personality is energized by other people at whatever cost. This personality seems to get very little accomplished, which is fine with them. They just want and need to be around people. They are not confrontational and are susceptible to peer-pressure. Many times, they will go against their own convictions in order to "go with the crowd." Peer approval is important to them and sought after.

People with high "I" tendencies influence others through talking and activity and tend to be emotional. They are described as convincing, magnetic, political, enthusiastic, persuasive, warm, demonstrative, trusting, and optimistic. For those with low "I" tendencies, they influence more by data and facts, and not with feelings. They are described as reflective, factual, calculating, skeptical, logical, suspicious, matter of fact, pessimistic, and critical. For the high "I," attention to detail and follow through is not important. Their charm and charisma can often lead them to take on many tasks, which may never actually get started— much less completed.

These people can become a strong leader through their natural ability to inspire. They also make great con men. An "I" is very spontaneous and thinks better "on their feet" than with a prepared speech. When leading "I" personalities, remember that recognition and praise are important to these people. Also, remember that when talking to an "I" personality, they are not really listening, but trying to figure out how to get back in control of the conversation. It may not be a conscious thought, but this is how that personality works. Instead of listening, they are thinking about what they want to say next.

Listening skills are NOT in their natural skill set; this needs to become a learned behavior. Leaders may have to repeat themselves often, write it down for them, and then have the "I" state back the task. They will remember every person they meet, but not what the discussion was about. Because of their ability to be flexible and spontaneous, they can quickly turn a situation to their favor and come out of the situation looking very good. They respond to pressure by becoming even more talkative and persuasive. To grow and mature, this person needs to temper inspiration with detail and must learn that others, besides themselves, have goals and influence. The "I" needs to remember: rather than looking inward and at what people can do for them, begin to look at other people and what they can do for others.

The "I" person must learn to esteem others even higher. As they invest in relationships that help others, they will find the greatest release for their inspiration and influence. As they grow and mature, they will shift away from what others can do for them and begin to think about what they can do for others. "I's" need to add task completion to their skill set, which will develop them into a strong and accomplished leader. The "I" has a natural ability to care for people, but not a natural ability to take care of tasks. Inspiration and influence are two of the most powerful tools available to become a great leader. People skills are their specialty. They have a tremendous ability to draw crowds together and motivate them to a higher purpose.

DISC Types: S—Steady and Stable

The "S" personality is always on everybody's "get-to-know" list. They provide the stability and backbone for any and all groups or organizations. These people hold the group together and are the easiest people to be around. Being the nicest people in the group, they are just enjoyable. They may seem to be quiet and shy at first, but they "warm up" once they get to know you.

While this personality is passive toward people, their value is immeasurable to the group. They may seem to be quiet and shy at first, but they really "warm up" once they get to know you. They will talk very little in the beginning stages of the group; however, once they are comfortable with people, they can talk non-stop. "S" personalities are easy to talk to and comfortable to be around. They want to know "who" is involved prior to

S

STEADY, STABLE & SUPPORTIVE

REFLECTIVE/PASSIVE/RESERVED & PEOPLE-ORIENTED

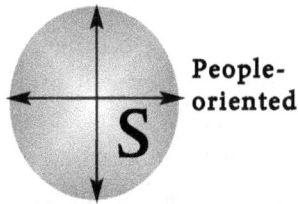

People-oriented

S

Reflective/Passive/Reserved

Greatest Strengths:
>Backbone of a group
>Working behind the scenes

Greatest Fear:
>Being alone

Greatest Challenge:
>Confrontation

Need to focus on:
>Standing up for what they believe
>Friendship isn't everything

committing to a task, project, party, or dinner. These people are the perfect balance to the look-at-me "I" personality because they prefer to talk to people behind the scenes. When the task or group runs into trouble spots, they calm everyone down and keep them focused and working together.

The "S" personality prefers people over tasks, but prefers to work one-on-one or in small groups. Many times the more active personalities, "D" and "I," will take the credit for much of the work done by the "S." However, that is fine with the "S;" they are not interested and would strongly prefer NOT to be in the limelight or get all the attention. Their quiet nature leads them to be thoughtful and intuitive people. People with high "S" traits want a steady pace, security, and do not like sudden changes. High "S" individuals are calm, relaxed, patient, possessive, predictable, deliberate, stable, consistent, and tend to be shy. In contrast, low "S" intensity traits are those who like change and variety. People with low "S" tendencies are described as restless, impatient, demonstrative, eager, or impulsive.

The "S" personalities are not strong task-oriented people; their strength is in looking out for others. They are much more interested in the general welfare of the people in the group rather than actually getting the work done which becomes the need of this personality. To be successful, it is important for them to acknowledge the task while working to keep the group together. To this personality group, it is all about their relationship with others. A wise leader will recognize this and "task" the "S" to work with the people of the group. Where the "I" is all about "me," the "S" is all about "you."

DISC Types: C—Cautious and Competent

The "C" personality team members are truly the people that get much of the actual work of a task or project done. The "C" personality is initially passive or reserved towards tasks; however, once organized the amount of work accomplished can be staggering. They prefer a checklist of items to be accomplished. The leader of the group may have to help these people with the list, but once it has been developed they will work tirelessly and efficiently in completing the list. The "C" traits demonstrate competence, compliance, and caution.

C

COMPETENT, COMPLIANT & CAUTIOUS

REFLECTIVE/PASSIVE/RESERVED & TASK-ORIENTED

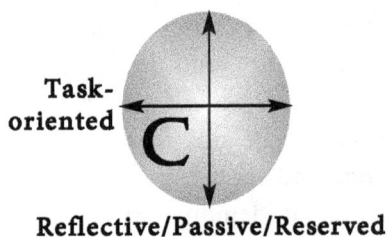

Task-oriented

C

Reflective/Passive/Reserved

Greatest Strengths:
     Accuracy
     Quality control

Greatest Fear:
     Being wrong

Greatest Challenges:
     Flexibility
     Taking risks

Need to focus on:
     Avoiding perfectionism
     Trust & faith

This is where much of the actual work gets done. While the "S" provides the glue, the "C" provides the substance and task completion for the group. The "C" personalities are not strong in relationships, but they are very strong in task completion. Most significant to the "C" traits is competency. Whereas, the "D" thinks they are always right, the "C" normally is always right. It is best not to disagree or contradict a "C" too quickly because you will most likely be apologizing soon.

"C" types are slow in making a decision, but once the decision is made it is virtually immutable. "C" personalities make great analysts. They will analyze something from every known angle and will even make up angles to study. This gives the appearance of being slow to decide, but to them all the facts are valuable and must be considered prior to making an accurate and lasting conclusion. People with high "C" styles adhere to rules, regulations, and structure. These people are good in quality control and compliance review. They like to do quality work and do it right the first time.

A "C" personality is known for being compliant which can by definition be seen as obedient, submissive, or yielding; however, this is not the "C" personality. It's important to understand that this personality is compliant, but it's being compliant to their own personal standards. If their standards differ from the company rules, it will be their standards that they follow. The "C" personality has built-in the ability to follow Shakespeare's admonition: "to thine own self be true"—regardless of circumstance or outside pressure. This is the single person in a jury who votes innocent when everyone else votes guilty; if they change their mind, it will be because they are absolutely convinced that they are wrong—not pressured into it. High "C" people are careful, cautious, exacting, neat, systematic, diplomatic, accurate, and tactful. Those with low "C" scores challenge the rules and want independence and are described as self-willed, stubborn, opinionated, arbitrary, unsystematic, and unconcerned with details.

DISC Style and Conflict

Much like death and taxes, conflict is a guaranteed part of life. It is not a question of IF conflict will come but WHEN. Many times, conflict may be the product of cultural values clashing. Elmer identifies that the Western use of "directness" may be beneficial in Western type cultures; however, in the non-Western cultures that make up the majority of the world, the direct/confrontational approach would be considered rude and immature (Elmer, 1993, p. 48). Global leaders must begin to hear what they are saying and try to understand what is actually being heard when they speak. Global leaders need to develop the personal skills of an active listener. Winston and Patterson defined active listening as the process of hearing the follower's emotions and intent as well as the spoken words (Winston & Patterson, 2006).

According to Stephen Covey, the fifth habit of highly effective people is to seek first to understand, then to be understood; this habit focuses on empathic or active listening which encourages people to listen with the intent of understanding before presenting their own information and opinions (Covey, 1989, p. 239). Active listening will help leaders understand themselves as well as gather information about other cultures. Over 5000 years ago, the great strategist Sun Tzu taught (The Denma Translation Group, 2003):

> If you know the enemy and know yourself, you need not fear the result of a hundred battles. If you know yourself but not the enemy, for every victory gained you will also suffer a defeat. If you know neither the enemy nor yourself, you will succumb in every battle.

Sun Tzu highlights the importance of knowing information about both sides in order to gain an advantage. As leaders practice the art of active listening, both sides gain an advantage.

Conflict has been around since the beginning of time. Gudykunst and Kim conclude that communication is the medium through which conflict is created and managed (Gudykunst & Kim, 2003, p. 296). Conflicts cannot be ignored. They must be resolved. According to Galbraith, organizational structure can generate its own levels of conflict and can easily produce more disagreements as well as confusion (Galbraith J. R., 2000, pp. 71-72). Bass concludes that in organizational life, a typical manager may spend up to

"D" Behavior—	"I" Behavior—
Under Pressure:	**Under Pressure:**
Becomes dictatorial, domineering, demanding, angry, intense, forceful, direct, bossy.	Becomes hyper, overly optimistic, immature, emotional, irrational, silly, wordy, selfish.
Sources of Irritation:	**Sources of Irritation:**
Weakness, indecisiveness, laziness, Lack of—discipline, plan, purpose, direction, authority, control, challenge.	Disinterest, slowness, pessimism, details, time restraints, antagonism, doubt, structure, lack of—enthusiasm, team participation.
Needs To:	**Needs To:**
Back off, seek peace, relax, think before reacting, control self, be—patient, loving, friendly, loyal, kind, sensitive.	Listen, count the cost, control emotions, be—humble, strong, disciplined, punctual, careful with words, conscientious.
"C" Behavior—	**"S" Behavior—**
Under Pressure:	**Under Pressure:**
Becomes moody, critical, contemplative, negative, worrisome.	Becomes subservient, insecure, fearful, weak-willed, withdrawn, sympathizer, sucker.
Sources of Irritation:	**Sources of Irritation:**
Incompetence, disorganization, foolishness, dishonesty, inaccuracy, wastefulness, inconsistency, blind faith, false impressions.	Pushiness, instability, inflexibility, anger, disloyalty, insensitivity, pride, discrimination, unfairness.
Needs To:	**Needs To:**
Loosen up, communicate, be—joyful, positive, tolerant, compromising, open, trusting, enthusiastic.	Be—strong, courageous, challenging, aggressive, assertive, confrontational, enthusaiastic, outgoing, expressive, cautious, bold.

25% of the organization's time dealing with conflicts which can be caused by many factors including organizational structure as well as personality driven conflict (Bass B., 2008, pp. 319-320). Left unresolved, personality conflicts may even lead faithful and diligent workers to leave an organization.

Often, the greatest hindrances to healthy relationships are personality conflicts. Positive individuals, desiring to build good relationships, are often discouraged because of misunderstandings and clashes with others. Personalities and conflict management resolution are designed to discover why people do what they do under pressure and why conflict occurs with others. Success in life principles on how to handle clashes is not always clear. The problem is many people are not aware of their "sensitive spots." Everyone needs to learn more about avoiding and resolving conflicts. Every personality has its "hot button." but should develop the measure for self-control through understanding others. The following are tendencies of personalities as they relate under pressure (Carbonell, 1993):

Understanding the differences between these styles makes it possible to identify the types of confrontational responses that each of these personality blends may demonstrate and how to respond to each. Most conflict is primarily the result of a miscommunication, frustration, and misunderstanding. Frustration is the product of un-met expectations; we expect people to act in a certain way, but they do not. With an understanding of the four basic personality types, conflict and frustration can be greatly reduced in an organization.

In response to personality-based conflict management and resolution, Carbonell has developed a Resolution Management Promise contract as a means of resolving personality-based organizational conflicts and suggests that organizations include this contract as a signed policy for all employees during their orientation period (Carbonell, 1993, pp. 119-120). This contract is based upon the principle of going first to the offended person alone and if that does not work then bring along a neutral individual to help mediate the conflict.

Leading with Style

If motivation represents why we do things, then style represents how we do things. Style can be a noun, verb, adjective or adverb and has the basic definition of a particular manner or technique by which something is done, created, or performed (Merriam-Webster.com, 2011). Replacing the word "something" in this definition with the word "leadership" would produce a definition of leadership style as a particular manner or technique by which leadership is done, created, or performed. Leadership style becomes how that leader accomplishes this definition. The essence of leadership is to get something done. How those things get done can vary from person to person.

With over seven billion people in the world and over seven billion unique plans for their lives, each person must be unique. Many times, leaders will see someone else and want to be like them. The problem with that is the other person has their own purpose, and duplicates are not usually needed. Each person has their own purpose and destiny.

What's Your Style?

There are lengthy commercial surveys available in the marketplace to help identify DISC leadership style and motivation; however, for all practical purposes, your leadership style determination only requires the answer to two questions:

- Outgoing or reserved in a leadership setting?
- Primarily interested in people or tasks?

Once these two questions have been answered, return to the matrix above and plot the answers to the correct quadrant. For example, if the answers were outgoing towards tasks, then quadrant "D" would be the leader and motivational style. This same model can be used to identify the rest of the team's style and motivation. Because each style and motivation is unique, a well-balanced team will have all four motivations represented; for example, the "D" sets the tasks, the "I" keeps the group working together, the "S" provides stability to the group, and the "C" provides a checklist needed to complete the task.

Leadership style and motivation work hand-in-hand as leaders interact with followers. Together, they provide the how and why of leaders' interaction. As leaders work toward understanding these components of leadership, they become better equipped as leaders. The unique expressions of the leadership style and motivation are an essential tool for a successful leader and organization.

Transactional and Transformational Personalities

Personalities in society and leadership tend to be described as being either transactional or transformational. Transactional leaders achieve set goals by acting within established procedures and standards. This leader assigns specific, well-defined tasks to subordinates and requires that they fulfill their responsibilities to meet the standards precisely as agreed upon. Transactional leadership emphasizes that the exchange that occurs between the leader and the follower is more directive in nature regarding the requirements and objectives (Bass B., 2008).

Reward and correction methods are based upon the "carrot and stick" approach. Rewards are contingent upon a successful completion of the "transaction". Meeting the objectives typically leads to rewards and reinforcement of the successful performance. The transactional rewards are primarily material (e.g. raise, award or "job security"). Corrective actions are typically more reactive than proactive—the leader monitors the deviations, mistakes and errors in the performance of the subordinates. Failure to reach the objectives will bring disappointment, dissatisfaction, and a psychological (e.g. negative feedback, disapproval, disciplinary actions), or material punishment (Bass B., 2008). Transformational leadership goes beyond just monitoring the performance of the followers and being reactive by providing negative feedback and corrective action when noticing an issue. It also puts a great emphasis on being proactive by establishing long- term goals, facilitating change, seeking continuous improvement, and giving the followers an opportunity to learn from their mistakes.

Unlike transactional leaders, transformational leaders achieve organizational goals by inspiring and motivating followers as well as encouraging their initiatives. Transformational leaders are able to establish a shared vision and sense of purpose among team members. Transformational leaders motivate their followers by raising their concerns from basic needs (e.g. security) to achievement and self-fulfillment; by moving them beyond self-interest to the concerns of the group, project or organization (Burns, 1978). They bring charisma, inspiration, intellectual stimulation, and individualized considerations (Bass B., 2008). Like transactional leadership, contingent rewards are present with transformational leadership and include both psychological and material ones (Bass B., 2008). Transformational leadership however, puts a great emphasis on the psychological rewards with the follower's self-actualization and rising above basic needs. Positive feedback and praise are also examples of psychological rewards.

Transformational leadership goes beyond just monitoring the performance of the followers and being reactive (providing negative feedback and corrective action when noticing an issue). It also puts a great emphasis on being proactive, establishing long-term goals, facilitating change, seeking continuous improvement, and giving the followers an opportunity to learn from their mistakes.

Any of the four DISC types of leaders can be transactional or transformational. In some cases, the situation may dictate the leadership style. However, the transformative personality will focus conflict resolution upon two main areas; renewing the mind, which encourages people in conflict to control their personality rather than having their personality control them and mentoring/discipling, which focuses upon people being able to understand the other person's behavior/response before trying to explain their own (Parsons, 2012, p. 92). After all, conflict cannot be ignored, it must be resolved. Developing an understanding and awareness of personality conflicts can be the first step in leaders developing their own personality and conflict management resolution program as well as establishing their transactional/transformational leadership style and understanding all members of their organization.

Chapter 12
Book Industry Innovation

"The key question isn't 'What fosters creativity?' But it is why in God's name isn't everyone creative? Where was the human potential lost? How was it crippled? I think therefore a good question might be not why do people create? But why do people not create or innovate? We have got to abandon that sense of amazement in the face of creativity, as if it were a miracle if anybody created anything."
—Abraham Maslow

"The world is but a canvas to the imagination."
—Henry David Thoreau

As emerging innovative leaders work to understand and develop the common core competencies, industry examples can also provide valuable insight into the innovative process. For example, the book industry has been hard-hit in the current economic times. Change is becoming the catalyst to produce new ways of doing business. The writing down of information has its foundation in the beginning of recorded history. From cave walls to clay tablets and from papyrus to paper, the writing of information has undergone many changes over the years. Innovation can be identified as the creative key for changes over time in this industry. As previously stated, innovation has been defined as the intentional development of a specific product, service, idea, environment, or process for the generation of value (Oster, 2011, p. 3). Value and relevance are key words for the continual evolution of the book industry. Publisher's Weekly reports that the number of publishers are declining and many bookstores are closing (Raugust, 2011). While the numbers of publishers are declining, the actual number of books in print had a modest 5% increase in 2010 according to Bowkers, the authoritative source for book publishers and books in print, with an estimated 316,480 books printed (Bowkers, 2011). However, change is once again on the horizon.

Utterback would categorize the book industry as waves of technological change with each change reflecting the fundamental objective but each change also represents a different way of achieving it (Utterback, 1996, pp. 18-19). Again, one of the oldest books ever written is *The Art of War*, which is a 7000 word "book" originally written on bamboo strips around 500 B.C. by the master strategist Sun Tzu (Michaelson, 2001). Stones could be the most ancient form of writing, but wood would be the first medium to take the guise of a book. From wood to paper to digital ink, books have survived over the years as the primary medium of communication (Encyclopedia Britannica, 2013).

Creativity

Innovation and creativity are closely linked. To release creativity requires seeing something different than everyone else. Albert Szent-Györgyi, a Hungarian-born biochemist who won the Nobel Prize in 1937, states that creativity and discovery consist of seeing what everybody has seen and thinking what nobody has thought (Szent-Gyorgyi, 1962). According to Oster, creativity requires a careful tending process, and everyone must be absolutely sure that wild and unusual ideas are welcomed as well as ensuring that any impediments to creativity are removed (Oster, 2011).

Perhaps the greatest challenge to releasing creativity is the stifling of the creative process that is required to think strategically. Businesses where creativity is not valued and nurtured will struggle to compete with more visionary enterprises because strategic leadership requires creativity in order to produce effective results (Strategic Direction, 2008). Cooper contends that creativity plays a vital role in the strategic thinking process in order to produce a sustained competitive advantage but also admits that many organizations actually discourage the freedom of practicing creativity (Cooper, 1998). Creative thinkers and innovators never seem to be corporate insiders much less those on the organizational fast track, and many times they need organizational cover from corporate fire since they do everything possible to escape the shackles of precedent, tradition, and orthodoxy (Oster, 2011).

Book Industry Innovation

According to Gryskiewicz, creativity and innovation have been found to be the cornerstone of healthy organizations that are ready for reinventing themselves, and organizations accomplish this by being relevant to changing markets as well as the use of new technology (Gryskiewicz, 1999, p. 1). Clay tablets were used in Mesopotamia in the 3rd millennium BC. The calamus, an instrument in the form of a triangle, was used to make characters in moist clay. The tablets were fired to dry them out. At Nineveh, 22,000 tablets were found, dating from the 7th century BC; this was the archive and library of the kings of Assyria, who had workshops of copyists and conservationists at their disposal. This presupposes a degree of organization with respect to books, consideration given to conservation, classification, etc. Tablets were used right up until the 19th century in various parts of the world, including Germany, Chile, and the Saharan Desert (Encyclopedia Britannica, 2013). Clay tablets eventually gave way to the use of papyrus.

After extracting the marrow from the papyrus stems, a series of steps (humidification, pressing, drying, gluing, and cutting), produced media of variable quality, the best being used for sacred writing. In Ancient Egypt, papyrus may have been used for writing as early as the First Dynasty, but the first evidence is from the account books of King Neferirkare Kakai of the Fifth Dynasty (Avrin, 1991, p. 83). A calamus made from the stem of a reed sharpened to a point, or bird feathers were used for writing. The script of Egyptian scribes was called hieratic or sacerdotal writing; it is not hieroglyphic, but a simplified form more adapted to manuscript writing (hieroglyphs usually being engraved or painted). Papyrus evolves into paper and remains the mainstay of books for centuries. However, innovation and creativity were not done with the book industry. The digital age dawns and books begin to embrace a digital format.

The Digital Age

According to a Strategic Study for the Book Publishing Industry in Ontario, forecasters do not see a collapse of physical books as a product, or of book publishing as an industry; however, it will become increasingly difficult to be competitive without adopting appropriate digital print processes, including digital distribution of content apart from the physical book (Castledale Inc, 2008). Offset printing has long been the printing method of choice for physical books. However, this process is slow, expensive, and difficult to change.

The advent of the digital press provides publishers with many more options. The concept is simple. Books are printed after they are ordered rather than before. This removes the need for pre-purchase cost of printing and warehouse storage space and fees. Changes or corrections to the book are quickly and inexpensively accomplished. Digital printing is also known as print-on-demand or POD printing. However, the POD industry is growing and maturing as well as addressing most of the quality issues of the past.

Publishers are also using this print option to keep titles in print longer, especially those selling less than 1,000 copies a year. The POD leader in the US, Lightning Source, now manufactures more than 1.3 million books per month and a few larger publishers in the US have purchased POD systems, which will print titles in their warehouse, one at a time, as they are sold (Thornton, 2008). This technology will only become more affordable in the next few years, allowing medium and smaller publishers to acquire POD systems or access to POD systems. This trend is also changing author agreements as "in print" and "out of print" definitions change.

Electronic Books Abound

According to the New York Times, eBooks and eReaders are upending the way books are published, sold, bought, and read as well as identifying that Barnes & Noble may be putting the future of the company in the hands of its eBook reader, the Nook (Bosman, 2012). With the new iPad, Apple is pushing their tablet deeper into the eBook race along with the Amazon

Kindle. Apple has sold nearly 40 million iPads since its debut in 2010 (Pepitone, 2011). While the iPad is not primarily an eBook Reader, Apple has its own eBook publishing standards that many publishers already use.

However, the Kindle and Nook are primarily eBook readers and the Kindle Fire, which is also a tablet, is reaching 5 million in sales (Pepitone, 2011). Barnes & Noble promotes that the Nook has over 2 million books available (Barnes & Noble, 2011). The Amazon Kindle store reports that 2,270,077 eBooks are available as of 11 October 2013 (Amazon, 2013). Book Business reported on an article written by Albert Greco of the Institute for Publishing Research that sales of print titles will drop from $18 billion in 2008 to $13.9 billion in 2015, and his projections show that e-book sales should increase to $3.6 billion by 2015 from $78 million in 2008 (Greco, 2011).

Innovation Forward

While format has changed over the years from writing on bamboo strips to a digital e-book, content still rules the publishing realm. Regardless of the format of a book, content is still the primary reason for consumers to purchase one. A Gallup poll identified that the primary reason consumers buy a book is for the subject (Woll, 2002). One analysis identifies that bookstores may not be the best place to sell a book due to the competition of other books available and concludes that placing the book in the proper market would be more effective (Bolme, 2006). Hence, even the placement and location to purchase the book has changed over time. Whereas most people might expect that the top reasons to buy books are book covers, marketing, price, reviews, etc., the 1996 Consumer Research Study on Book Publishing reports that the number one reason that consumers purchase a book is the subject of the book (American Booksellers Association, 1996).

Innovations are not unique to the book publishing business as they are sweeping across most industries. In a time of unpredictability, innovation opens the doors to new opportunities for those that are prepared. Working to develop these common core competencies will help emerging innovative leaders be prepared to step-up with new ideas for old systems.

Chapter 13
Leadership Continues

"There is nothing more difficult to take in hand,
more perilous to conduct, or more uncertain in
its success, than to take the lead in the introduction
of a new order of things."
—Niccolo Machiavelli

"If your actions inspire others to dream more, learn more,
do more and become more, you are a leader."
—John Quincy Adams

Leadership has been around since the beginning of time, and is as old as time itself. Therefore, the journey to identify common core competencies of innovation leadership should start at the beginning. While the concept of innovative leadership may be a relatively new topic, leadership has existed for millennia, and many works have stood the test of time for leadership development.

4500 Year Old Leadership Principles Still Work

Perhaps the oldest and most complete literary work on leadership may be *The Instruction of Ptah-Hotep*, which was written during the Fifth Egyptian Dynasty and dates from approximately 2495 to 2345 B.C. This papyrus relays the rules of behavior that all wise men should pass to their children and contains 50 maxims to live and govern by according to Ptah-Hotep, the Vizier of Egypt. These maxims included the following examples (Gunn, 2004):

1. Set a Good Example
2. Follow the Path of Truth
3. Be Kind and Receive Kindness in Return
4. Be Industrious, Fair to Your Neighbors and Pay Your Taxes
5. The Blessing of Children
6. Honor the Advancement of Others and Serve a Wise Man
7. Work Hard, Be Not Slothful
8. Take Time to Refresh Your Spirit
9. Love Your Neighbor and You will Prosper
10. Be Not Covetous with Your Neighbors
11. Cherish Your Wife
12. Guard Your Reputation

The Sun Tzu of Leadership

Sun Tzu may be considered the "Ptah-Hotep" of China. In approximately 500 B.C., the military leaders under the command of Sun Tzu put their collective wisdom into written form, and their 7000 word text was to shape the strategic thinking of all Asia in what is commonly called *The Art of War.* (The Denma Translation Group, 2003, p. 1). This text is still studied by military strategists and leaders around the world as well as at every military academy in the United States.

Former U.S. Chairman of the Joint Chiefs of Staff General Colin Powell said, "I've read the Chinese classic *The Art of War* written by Sun Tzu. He has been studied for hundreds of years and continues to give inspiration to soldiers and politicians. So every American soldier in the army knows of his works. We require our soldiers to read it (McNeilly, 1996, p. 73)." *The Art of War* is not just for military leaders. According to Michaelson, the lessons of Sun Tzu can be applied to real-life situations and serve as an everyday resource for all kinds of strategic thought especially strategic issues for business leaders and managers (Michaelson, 2001, pp. xx-xxi). Since the beginning of time, leadership principles have been used and passed down to other generations. Yet, efforts to identify a common core of competencies seem to be in its infancy for emerging innovative leaders.

However, proper study of any text requires an exegetical method of analysis. The Socio-Rhetorical Interpretation espoused by Vernon K. Robbins provides an outstanding tool for analysis because the focus is on the language itself. Rhetorical analysis is a method of close reading (criticism) that employs the principles of rhetoric to examine the interactions between a text, an author, and an audience. The focus is more on what the text "does" than what it "is". This type of analysis may be performed against any text or image. Therefore, it serves as a valuable tool for research and analysis in the hands of innovative leaders. Robbins identifies five different angles to explore multiple textures within texts in his Socio-Rhetorical Interpretation model (Robbins, 1996, pp. 3-4):

1. Inner Texture has features like the repetition of particular words, the creation of beginnings and endings, alternation of speech and storytelling, particular ways in which the words present arguments, and the particular feel or aesthetic of the text. This focus is on the language itself and uses six types of inner texture analyses to discover patterns. The six types of inner texture analyses and patterns are the repetitive texture and pattern, progressive texture and pattern, narrational texture and pattern, argumentative texture and pattern, opening-middle-closing texture and pattern, and the sensory-aesthetic texture and pattern.

2. Intertexture concerns a text's configuration of phenomena that lie outside the text. A major goal of Intertextual analysis is to ascertain the nature and result of processes of configuration and reconfiguration of phenomena in the world outside the text from four patterns; the Oral-Scribal Intertexture, Cultural Intertexture, Social Intertexture, and Historical Intertexture.

3. Social and cultural texture—not to be confused with social and cultural inter-texture—concerns the capacities of the text to support social reform, withdrawal, or opposition and to evoke cultural perceptions of dominance, subordinance, difference, or exclusions. Specific social topics in the text exhibit resources for changing people or social practices, for destroying and re-creating social order, for withdrawing from present society to create one's

own social world, or for coping with the world by transforming one's own perceptions of it.

4.   Ideological texture begins with people, and defines ideology as an integrated system of beliefs, assumptions, and values. It is concerned with the alliance and conflicts within the language of the text as well as the way the text, and its interpreters, position themselves relative to other individuals and groups in that time. The individual locations sub-texture is the first step toward ideological texture analysis. It is characterized by the individuals' involved in the text responses to the world as well as the individuals' cultural location. Robbins uses the ideological texture to focus on the socio-cultural background and individual location as well as the perspective of the writers and readers of the text. DeSilva identifies that ideological texture recognizes that a text is not just a vehicle for ideas but rather a vehicle by which the author hopes to achieve a certain goal (DeSilva, 2004, p. 25).

5.   Sacred texture analysis describes a systemic and creative study of Scripture that provides insights regarding the nature of the relationship between divine life and human life. Shillington indicates that sacred texture refers to biblical text from a religious community to a religious community, and when complemented with theological interpretation yields valuable results (Shillington, 2002, p. 279).

Through the use of the Socio-Rhetorical Interpretation, proper analysis and exposition of any text can be made accessible for innovative leaders. Whether a captain of ten or a captain of thousands, relying only on natural leadership abilities is unwise and limiting. A strategic plan for developing innovative leaders determines to develop leaders in our changing world. As Mahatma Gandhi said, "We must become the change we want to see." Academies must educate, organizations must invest, and individuals must heed the charge to develop these common cores or competencies to emerge as innovative leaders:

1. Creativity
2. Strategic Mindset
3. Redesign
4. Trust & Ethics
5. Context
6. Forecasting
7. Rest & Renewal
8. Leadership Succession
9. Mentoring/Discipling
10. Understanding People

Again, this list is not comprehensive but, at least, identifies a starting point to begin the process for emerging leaders to develop in the quest to become an innovative leader. These common cores or competencies for emerging innovative leaders can be used to establish and fortify the force of change in our human culture. Success of an individual has not always assured the success of an organization; however, with these core characteristics, individual leadership success will be assured in conjunction with organizational success. With a level of proficiency in these aptitudes, change can be embraced, and evolution for impact on the future will be guaranteed.

About the Author

DARRELL PARSONS is a military officer, educator, and businessman. He holds a Doctorate Degree in Strategic Leadership and Innovation from the Regent University School of Business and Leadership. Dr. Parsons currently holds a faculty position at Radford University in Radford, Virginia.

Through Leadership Development International (LDI), Dr. Parsons is a demonstrated leader in providing thought leadership in the area of innovation through his InnovateNOW™ Leadership Development Program. LDI is a consulting organization dedicated to helping organizations develop leaders around the world. Dr. Parsons is also a DISC Certified Human Behavioral Consultant through the Leadership Institute of America, and he provides leadership training seminars to help organizations develop personality-based leadership programs. Further information can be found at www.LDIweb.com.

With over 27 years of military experience, Dr. Parsons has provided leadership expertise throughout the Department of Defense to include the Chairman of the Joint Chiefs of Staff. He and his wife, Diane Parsons, founded Parsons Publishing House in 2007 and GLE Books in 2014. As a veteran author, this book follows the publishing of *Release Your Words—Impact Your World* and *Why Do I Do the Things I Do?—Understanding Personalities.*

More information about Parsons Publishing House can be found at www.ParsonsPublishingHouse.com.

For speaking or publishing questions, Dr. Parsons may be contacted at Darrell@ParsonsPublishingHouse.com.

References

Aaltio-Marjosola, I., & Takala, T. (2000). Charismatic Leadership, Manipulation and the Complexity of Organizational Life. *Journal of Workplace Learning*, 12(4), 146-158 DOI: 10.1108/13665620010332750.

Air Force Times. (2004). Retrieved August 1, 2011, from http://www.airforcetimes.com/legacy/new/0-AIRPAPER-487000.php

Amazon. (2013). Retrieved October 11, 2013, from http://www.amazon.com/s/ref=nb_sb_noss?url=search-alias%3Ddigital-text&field-keywords=

American Booksellers Association. (1996). *The 1996 Consumer Research Study on Book Publishing*. New York: American Booksellers Association.

Appelbaum, S. H., St-Pierre, N., & Glavas, W. (1998). Strategic Organizational Change: The Role of Leadership, Learning, Motivation and Productivity. *Management Decision*, 36(5), 289 -301 DOI: 10.1108/00251749810220496.

Ashkenas, R., Ulrich, D., Jick, T., & Kerr, S. (2002). *The Boundaryless Organization: Breaking the Chains of Organizational Structure*. San Francisco: Jossey-Bass.

Avrin, L. (1991). Scribes, Script and Books: The Book Arts from Antiquity to the Renaissance. New York: American Library Association.

Baez-Camargo, G. (1986). *Archaeological Commentary on the Bible*. New York: Doubleday-Galilee Books.

Barnes & Noble. (2011). Retrieved October 11, 2013, from http://bookclubs.barnesandnoble.com/t5/NOOK-Color-General-Discussion/B-amp-N-Says-There-Are-Over-2-Million-Books-Available/td-p/790676

Bass, B. (1990). From Transactional to Transformational Leadership: Learning to Share the Vision. *Organizational Dynamics*, 18(3), 19-31.

Bass, B. (2008). *The Bass Handbook of Leadership*. New York: Free Press.

Bell, C. R. (2002). *Managers as Mentors*. San Francisco: Berrett-Koehler Publishers Inc.

Bell, M., & Tunnicliff, G. (1996). Future Search for Stakeholders. *Management Development Review*, 9(1), 13-16.

Bennis, W. (1999). The End of Leadership: Exemplary Leadership Is Impossible without Full Inclusion, Initiatives, and Cooperation of Followers. *Organizational Dynamics*, 28(1), 71-79 DOI: 10.1016/S0090-2616(00)80008-X.

Bennis, W. (2000). Breaking the Code of Change. (M. Beer, & N. Nohria, Eds.) Cambridge: Harvard Business School.

Bennis, W. G. (1992). *On Becoming a Leader.* Wilmington: Addison-Wesley.

Bingham, T., & Galagan, P. (2010). Be More Innovative: An Interview with Dan Cathy. T+D, 64(3), 36-41.

Black, J. S., Morrison, A. J., & Gregersen, H. B. (1999). *Global Explorers: The Next Generation of Leaders.* New York: Routledge.

Blackaby, H. T., & Blackaby, R. (2001). *Spiritual Leadership.* Nashville: Broadman and Holman Publishers.

Block, P. (2001). *The Flawless Consutling Fieldbook and Companion.* San Francisco: Jossey-Bass/Pfeiffer.

Bloom, B. S. (1971). *Mastery Learning: Theory and Practice.* New York City: Holt Rinehart & Winston.

Bolme, S. (2006). *Your Guide to Marketing Books in the Christian Marketplace.* Charlotte: Crest Publications.

Bosman, J. (2012). *NY Times.* Retrieved October 11, 2013, from http://www.nytimes.com/2012/01/29/business/barnes-noble-taking-on-amazon-in-the-fight-of-its life.html?_r=4&pagewanted=all?src=tp

Bossidy, L., & Charan, R. (2002). Execution: *The Discipline of Getting Things Done.* New York: Crown Publishing Group.

Bowkers. (2011). *Bowker's Annual Book Production Report.* New Providence: Bowkers.

Branson, C. M. (2009). *Leadership for an Age of Wisdom.* New York: Springer Science+Business Media.

Brown, M. (1989). Ethics in Organizations . *Issues in Ethic*, 2(1), 3-6.

Buckler, B. (1996). A Learning Process Model to Achieve Continuous Improvement and Innovation. The Learning Organization, 3(3), 31–39.

Burns, J. M. (1978). *Leadership.* New York: Harper& Row.

BusinessDictionary.com. (2012). Retrieved June 13, 2012, from http://www.businessdictionary.com/definition/gatekeeper.html

Cameron, K. S., & Quinn, R. E. (2011). *Diagnosing and Changing Organizational Culture Based on the Competing Values Framework* (3rd ed.). San Francisco: Jossey-Bass.

References

Canton, J. (2006). *The Extreme Future: The Top Trends that will Reshape the World for the next 5, 10, and 20 Years.* New York: Dutton.

Carbonell, M. (1993). *Solving the Mystery of Motivation.* Fayetteville, GA: Institute of Leadership Technology.

Castledale Inc. (2008). *A Strategic Study for the Book Publishing Industry in Ontario.* Ontario, Canada: Castledale Inc.

Cheng, C. (1998). Uniform Change: An Ethnography on Organizational Symbolism, Volunteer Motivation and Dysfunctional Change in a Paramilitary Organization. *Leadership & Organization Development Journal,* 19(1), 22-31 DOI: 10.1108/01437739810368802.

Chermack, T. J. (2011). *Scenario Planning in Organizations.* San Francisco: Berrett-Koehler Publishers, Inc.

Ciulla, J. (Ed.). (2004). *Ethics, the Heart of Leadership.* Westport: Praeger Publishers.

Cockerell, L. (2008). *Creating Magic: 10 Common Sense Leadership Strategies from a Life at Disney.* New York: Doubleday.

Cohen, S. L. (2010). Effective Global Leadership Requires a Global Mindset. *Industrial and Commercial Training,* 42(1), 3-10.

Cohen, W. A. (1998). *The Stuff of Heroes: The Eight Universal Laws of Leadership.* Marietta, GA: Longstreet.

Cooper, J. R. (1998). A Multidimensional Approach to the Adoption of Innovation. Management Decision, 36(8), 493-502 DOI: 10.1108/00251749810232565.

Cornish, E. (2005). *Futuring: The Exploration of the Future.* Bethesda: World Future Society.

Covey, S. (1989). *The 7 Habits of Highly Effective People.* New York, NY: Fireside.

Daft, R. L. (2007). *Organization Theory and Design* (9th ed.). Mason, OH: Thomson South-Western.

Darling, J. R., & Heller, V. L. (2011). Managing Conflict with the Chinese: The Key from an In-Depth Single Case Study. *Chinese Management Studies,* 5(1), 35-54 DO: 10.1108/17506141111118444.

de Kluyver, C. A., & Pearce II, J. A. (2012). *Strategy: A View from the Top.* Upper Saddle River, NJ: Pearson Education Inc.

Deming, W. E. (1994). *The New Economics For Industry, Government, Education* (2 ed.). Cambridge: Massachusetts Institute of Technology.

DeSilva, D. A. (2004). *An Introduction to the New Testament Contexts, Methods & Ministry Formation.* Downers Grove: InterVarsity Press.

Disney Institute. (2001). *Be Our Guest.* New York: Disney Editions.

Dolan, S. L., & Richley, B. A. (2006). Management by Values (MBV): A New Philosophy for a New Economic Order. *Handbook of Business Strategy,* 7(1), 235-238 DOI: 10.1108/10775730610618873.

Eisner, M. (1999). *A Work in Progress.* London: Penguin Books.

Elmer, D. (1993). *Cross-Cultural Conflict: Building Relationships for Effective Ministry.* Downers Grove: InterVarsity Press.

Elmuti, D., & Kathawala, Y. (2001). An Overview of Strategic Alliances. *Management Decision,* 39(3), 205-218 DOI: 10.1108/EUM0000000005452.

Emerald Group Publishing. (2011). Joint Effort: Integrating Leadership Development and Organizational Change. *Strategic Direction,* 27(1), 18-20 DOI: 10.1108/02580541111096566.

Encyclopedia Britannica. (2013). Retrieved October 1, 2013, from http://www.britannica.com/EBchecked/topic/482597/history-of-publishing/28597/Book-publishing

Finzel, H. (1994). *The Top Ten Mistakes Leaders Make.* Wheaton, IL: Victor Books.

Fletcher, B., & Jones, F. (1992). Measuring Organizational Culture: The Cultural Audit. *Managerial Auditing Journal,* 7(6), 30-37.

Foreman, K. (1999). Evolving Global Structures and the Challenges Facing International Relief and Development Organizations. *Nonprofit and Voluntary Sector Quarterly,* 28(4), 178–197.

Frynas, J. G. (1998). Political Instability and Business: Focus on Shell in Nigeria. *Third World Quarterly,* 19(3), 457-478 DOI:10.1080/01436599814343.

Fua, S. J. (2007). Looking Towards the Source – Social Justice and Leadership Conceptualisations from Tonga. *Journal of Educational Administration,* 45(6), 672-683 DOI: 10.1108/09578230710829865.

Fuller, B. (1975). *Synergetics—Explorations in the Geometry of Thinking.* New York: Macmillan Publishing.

Gabler, N. (2007). *Walt Disney.* New York: Vintage Books.

Gabrielsson, J., & Politis, D. (2009). Entrepreneurs' Attitudes Towards Failure: An Experiential Learning Approach. *International Journal of Entrepreneurial Behaviour & Research,* 15(4), 364 - 383 DOI: 10.1108/13552550910967921.

Galbraith, J. (2002). *Designing Organizations: An Executive Guide to Strategy, Structure, and Process.* San Francisco: Jossey-Bass.

References

Galbraith, J. R. (2000). *Designing the Global Corporation*. San Francisco: John Wiley & Sons, Inc.

Garavan, T. N., & Deegan, J. (1995). Discontinuous Change in Organizations: Using Training and Development Interventions to Develop Creativity. *Industrial and Commercial Training*, 27(11), 18-25 DOI: 10.1108/00197859510147607.

Gary, J. (2008). The Future According to Jesus: A Galilean Model of Foresight. *Futures*, 40(7), 630-642 DOI:10.1016/j.futures.2007.12.004.

George, B. (2007). *True North: Discover Your Authentic Leadership*. San Francisco: Jossey-Bass.

Ghislanzoni, G., Heidari-Robinson, S., & Jermiin, M. (December 2010). Taking Organizational Redesigns from Plan to Practice. *McKinsey Quarterly*, 1-9.

Graham, R. (1981). The Role of Perception of Time in Consumer Research. *Journal of Consumer Research*(7), 335-342.

Greco, A. (2011). *Book Business*. Retrieved October 5, 2013, from http://www.bookbusinessmag.com/article/ebooks-by-numbers/1

Greenberger, D., & Thoms, P. (1995). The Relationship Between Leadership and Time Orientation. *Journal of Management Inquiry*, 4(3), 272-292.

Gregson, K. (1994). Mentoring. *Journal of Workplace Learning*, 6(4), 26-27 DOI: 10.1108/13665629410071225.

Grocock, A. (2002). Universities in the Future. *Journal of the Royal Society of Medicine*, 95(1), 48-49.

Gryskiewicz, S. (1999). *Positive Turbulence: Developing Climates for Creativity, Innovation, and Renewal*. San Francisco: Jossey Bass.

Gudykunst, W. B., & Kim, Y. Y. (2003). *Communicating with Strangers*. New York: McGraw-Hill.

Gunn, B. G. (2004). *Instructions of Ptah Hotep*. Retrieved July 1, 2014, from http://www.kenseamedia.com/encyclopedia/ppp/instructions_ptah_hotep.htm.

Gupta, A. (2008). International Trends and Private Higher Education in India. *International Journal of Educational Management*, 22(6), 565-594 DOI: 10.1108/09513540810895462.

Gyertson, D. J. (Ed.). (1993). *Salt & Light: A Christian Response to Current Issues*. Dallas: Word Publishing.

Hall, E. (1976). *Beyond Culture*. New York: Anchor Books.

Hall, E. (1989). *Beyond Culture*. New York: Anchor Press.

Hamel, G. (2000). *Leading the Revolution*. Boston: Harvard Business School Press.

Harrison, E. F. (1995). Strategic Planning Maturities. *Management Decision*, 33(2), 48-55.

Hauschildt, J., & Schewe, G. (2000). Gatekeeper and Process Promotor: Key Persons in Agile and Innovative Organizations. *International Journal of Agile Management Systems*, 2(2), 96-103 DOI: 10.1108/14654650010312624.

Hendricks, H. G., & Hendricks, W. D. (1995). *As Iron Sharpens Iron*. Chicago: Moody Press.

Heracleos, L. (1998). Strategic Thinking or Strategic Planning. *Long Range Planning*, 31(3), 481-487.

Hersey, P., & Blanchard, K. (1969). Life cycle theory of leadership. *Training & Development Journal*, Vol 23(5), 26-34.

Hines, A. (2006). Strategic Foresight. *The Futurist*(September- October), 18-21.

Hines, A., & Bishop, P. (Eds.). (2006). *Thinking About the Future: Guidelines for Strategic Foresight*. Washington: Social Technologies, LLC.

Ho, V. L., & Sculli, D. (1998). The Strategic Insights of Sun Tzu and Quality Management. *The TQM Magazine*, 10(3), 161 - 168 DOI: 10.1108/09544789810214774.

Hofstede, G. (1984). *Culture's Consequences: International Differences in Work Related Values*. Newbury Park: SAGE Publications Inc.

Hofstede, G. (1993). Cultural Constraints in Management Theories. *The Executive*, 7(1), 81-94.

Hofstede, G. (2001). *Culture's Consequences* (2nd ed.). Thousand Oaks: Sage.

Houghton, J. D., & DiLiello, T. C. (2010). Leadership Development: The Key to Unlocking Individual Creativity in Organizations. *Leadership & Organization Development Journal*, 31(3), 230 - 245 DOI: 10.1108/01437731011039343.

Hughes, R. L., & Beatty, K. C. (2005). *Becoming A Strategic Leader: Your Role in Your Organization's Enduring Success*. San Francisco: Jossey-Bass.

Hunter, S., Steinberg, P., & Taylor, M. (2012). *Shifting to a Strategy of Innovation: The Key Role of Leadership in Consumer Packaged Goods*. State College: Penn State Executive Program.

Irvine, G. (1996). *Best Things in the Worst Times: An Insiders View of World Vision*. Wilsonville, Oregon: BookPartners, Inc.

References

Isherwood, A. (2011). *Strategy Tool Usage: What Tools Do Practicing Managers Use?* Retrieved February 16, 2012, from http://www.aiconsortia.com/documents/strategy-tool-usage-survey.pdf

Jarzabkowski, P., Giulietti, M., & Oliveira, B. (2011). *Advanced Institute of Management Research.* Retrieved October 16, 2013, from http://www.aimresearch.org/uploads/File/Publications/Executive%20Briefings%202/Building_a_strategy_toolkit.pdf

Joas, H. (2000). *The Genesis of Values.* Chicago: University of Chicago Press.

Johanson, U., Skoog, M., Backlund, A., & Almqvist, R. (2006). Balancing Dilemmas of the Balanced Scorecard. *Accounting, Auditing & Accountability Journal,* 19(6), 842-857 DOI: 10.1108/09513570610709890.

Jones, R. (2010). *Army MWR.* Retrieved August 1, 2011, from http://www.armymwr.com/UserFiles/file/Commander/Travel_Guide-5_4c.pdf

Joseph, E. E., & Winston, B. E. (2005). A Correlation of Servant Leadership, Leader Trust, and Organizational Trust. *Leadership & Organization Development Journal,* 26(1), 6 - 22 DOI: 10.1108/01437730510575552.

Kaniss, A. (2006). Achieving a good P/PC balance. *Comprint Military Publications,* 3-4.

Kaplan, R., & Norton, D. (2001). The Strategy-Focused Organization. *Strategy & Leadership,* 29(3), 41-2.

Keidel, R. W. (1995). *Seeing Organizational Patterns.* San Francisco: Berrett-Koehler Publishers.

Khurana, R. (2002). *Searching for a Corporate Savior: The Irrational Quest for Charismatic CEOs.* Princeton: Princeton Press.

Kotter, J. P. (2005). Change Leadership. Leadership Excellence, 22(12), 3-4.

Kouzes, J. M., & Posner, B. Z. (1993). *Credibility: How Leaders Gain and Lose It, Why People Demand It.* San Francisco: Jossey-Bass Inc.

Kuczmarski, S. S., & Kuczmarski, T. D. (1995). *Values-Based Leadership.* Englewood Cliffs: Prentice Hall.

LaChance, S. (2006). Applying the Balanced Scorecard. *Strategic HR Review,* 5(2), 7.

LaHaye, T. (1983). *Transformed Temperaments.* Wheaton, IL: Tyndale House Publishers.

Lam, Y. (2002). Defining the Effects of Transformational Leadership on Organisational Learning: A Cross-Cultural Comparison. : *School Leadership and Management*, 22(4), 439-452 DOI: 10.1080/1363243022000053448.

Leadership Talks. (2007). Retrieved July 7, 2014, from http://www.regent.edu/admin/media/mp3/schgle/mentoring_discipli ng.mp3.

Lehn, K., & Makhija, A. K. (1996). EVA & MVA as Performance Measures and Signals for Strategic Change. *Strategy & Leadership*, 24(3), 15-16.

Littauer, F., & Littauer, M. (2006). *Communication Plus*. Ventura, CA: Regal Books.

Liu, C., Yu, Z., & Tjosvold, D. (2002). Production and People Values: Their Impact on Relationships and Leader Effectiveness in China. *Leadership & Organization Development Journal*, 23(3), 134-144 DOI: 10.1108/01437730210424075.

Locke, E. A., & Jain, V. K. (1995). Organizational Learning and Continuous Improvement. *International Journal of Organizational Analysis*, 3(1), 45-68 DOI:10.1108/eb028823.

Loo, T. (2006). *How to Define Your Life Purpose*. Retrieved September 3, 2013, from http://ezinearticles.com/?How-to-Define-Your-Life-Purpose&id=331527.

Madichie, N. (2011). The Darfur Conflict – Geography or Institutions? *Management Decision*, 49(7), 1214-1216.

Marquardt, M. J., & Berger, N. O. (2000). *Global Leaders for the 21st Century* . Albany: State University of New York Press.

Marren, P. (2010). Nailing Strategic Jello to the Wall. *Journal of Business Strategy*, 31(3), 59 - 61 DOI: 10.1108/02756661011036727.

Maslach, C., & Leiter, M. (1997). *The Truth About Burnout: How Organizations Cause Personal Stress and What To Do About It*. San Francisco: Jossey-Bass.

Mason, J. (1993). *You're Born an Orginal Don't Die a Copy*. Tulsa, OK: Insight International.

May, S. (Ed.). (2012). *Case Studies in Organizational Communication: Ethical Perspectives and Practices* (2 ed.). Thousand Oaks: SAGE Publications, Inc .

McCall Jr., M. W., & Hollenbeck, G. P. (2002). *Developing Global Executives* . Boston: Harvard Business School Publishing.

References

McEntire, L. E., & Greene-Shortridge, T. M. (2011). Recruiting and Selecting Leaders for Innovation: How to Find the Right Leader. *Advances in Developing Human Resources*(13), 266- 278.

McKinney, M. (2011). *Choosing Service Over Self-Interest: The Focus of Leadership*. Retrieved January 10, 2014, from http://www.leadershipnow.com/service.html

McNeilly, M. (1996). *Sun Tzu and the Art of Business*. New York: Oxford University Press.

Merriam-Webster.com. (2011). Retrieved July 23, 2011, from http://www.merriam-webster.com/dictionary/style

Michaelson, G. A. (2001). *The Art of War for Managers: 50 Strategic Rules*. Avon: Adams Media Corporation.

Miller, C. (1995). *The Empowered Leader*. Nashville, TN: Broadman & Holman Publishers.

Mintzberg, H. (1994). *Rise and Fall of Strategic Planning* . New York: Free Press.

Mintzberg, H., Ahlstrand, B., & Lampel, J. (2005). *Strategy Safari: A Guided Tour Through the Wilds of Strategic Management*. New York: Free Press.

Mitleton-Kelly, E. (2013). *What are the Characteristics of a Learning Organization?* Retrieved from GEMI Metrics Navigator: http://www.gemi.org/metricsnavigator/eag/What%20are%20the%20 Characteristics%20of%20a%20Learning%20Organization.pdf

Morden, T. (1999). Models of National Culture—A Management Review. *Cross Cultural Management: An International Journal*, 6(1), 19-44 DOI: 10.1108/13527609910796915.

Morgan, G. (1997). *Images of Organization* (2nd ed.). Thousand Oaks, CA: Sage Publications Inc.

Morrison, T., & Conaway, W. A. (2006). *Kiss, Bow or Shake Hands*. Avon, MA: Adams Media.

Mumford, M. D., Scott, G. M., Gaddis, B., & Strange, J. M. (2002). Leading Creative People: Orchestrating Expertise and Relationships. *The Leadership Quarterly*(13), 705 – 750.

Nadler, D. A., & Tushman, M. L. (1997). *Competing by Design: The Power of Organizational Architecture*. New York: Oxford University Press.

New Media Consortium. (2012). *Horizon Report: 2012 Higher Education Edition*. Retrieved October 31, 2013, from http://www.nmc.org/system/files/pubs/1328995195/2012-Horizon-Report-HE.pdf

Northouse, P. G. (2007). *Leadership Theory and Practice* (4th ed.). Thousand Oaks, CA: Sage Publications, Inc.

Oguz, F., & Sengün, A. E. (2011). Mystery of the Unknown: Revisiting Tacit Knowledge in the Organizational Literature. *Journal of Knowledge Management,* 15(3), 445-461 DOI: 10.1108/13673271111137420.

Olivares, O. J. (2011). The Formative Capacity of Momentous Events and Leadership Development. *Leadership & Organization Development Journal,* 32(8), 837-853 DOI: 10.1108/01437731111183766.

Oliver, R. W. (1999). Real Time Strategy: Strategy as Sports! War!... Food? *Journal of Business Strategy,* 20(5), 8 - 10 DOI: 10.1108/eb040022 .

O'Neil, J. R. (1993). *The Paradox of Success: A Book of Renewal for Leaders.* New York: Penguin Putnam Books.

Oster, G. W. (2011). *The Light Prize: Perspectives on Christian Innovation.* Virginia Beach, VA: Positive Signs Media.

Palaima, T., & Skaržauskiene, A. (2010). Systems Thinking as a Platform for Leadership Performance in a Complex World. *Baltic Journal of Management,* 5(3), 330-355 DOI: 10.1108/17465261011079749.

Parsons, D. (2007). *Release Your Words: Impact Your World.* Panama City: Parsons Publishing House.

Parsons, D. (2012). *Why Do I Do the Things I Do?* Stafford: Parsons Publishing House.

Pepitone, J. (2011). *CNN Money.* Retrieved October 6, 2013, from http://money.cnn.com/2011/12/15/technology/amazon_kindle_sales/index.htm

Peters, T. (1978). *Futures: Human and Divine.* Atlanta: John Knox Press.

Pfeffer, J. (1998). *The Human Equation Buiding Profits by Putting People First.* Boston: Harvard Business School Press.

Pillemer, D. B.-1. (2011). Pillemer, D. B. *Momentous Events in the Life Story,* 5, 122-134.

Pisapia, J., Reyes-Guerra, D., & Coukos-Semmel, E. (2005). Developing the Leader's Strategic Mindset: Establishing the Measures. Kravis *Leadership Institute, Leadership Review,* 5(Spring), 41-68.

Puryear, E. F. (2002). *American Generalship- Character is Everything: The Art of Command.* Novato, CA: Presidio Press Inc.

Rath, T. (2007). *Strengths Finder 2.0.* New York: Gallup Press.

References

Raugust, K. (2011). *Publishers Weekly*. Retrieved October 10, 2013, from http://www.publishersweekly.com/pw/by-topic/childrens/childrens-industry-news/article/46267-toy-fair-2010-number-of-publishers-declines-but-children--s-books-still-have-presence.html

Rausch, E. (1996). Guidelines for Participation in Appropriate Decision Making. *Management Development Review*, 9(4), 29-34 DOI: 10.1108/09622519610123751.

Relative, S. (2008). Retrieved July 9, 2013, from http://voices.yahoo.com/fly-like-eagle-steve-miller-band-song-all-865301.html?cat=33

Robbins, V. K. (1996). *Exploring the Texture of Texts A Guide to Socio-Rhetorical Interpretation*. Harrisburg: Trinity Press International.

Rodica, M. B. (2009). The Balanced Scorecard In A Strategy-Focused Organization. *Romania Proceedings* (pp. 79-89). Thessaloniki, Greece: Association of Economic Universities of South and Eastern Europe and the Black Sea Region.

Rorty, R. (1989). *Contingency, Irony, and Solidarity*. Cambridge: Cambridge University Press.

Rorty, R. (1999). *Philosophy and Social Hope*. London: Penguin Books.

Rothwell, W. J. (2005). *Effective Succession Planning 3rd Edition: Ensuring Leadership Continuity and Building Talent from Within*. New York: American Management Association.

Sanchez-Bueno, M. J., & Suarez-Gonzalez, I. (2010). Towards New Organizational Forms. *International Journal of Organizational Analysis*, 18(3), 340 - 357 DOI: 10.1108/19348831011062166.

Sanders, T. I. (1998). *Strategic Thinking and the New Science: Planning in the Midst of Chaos, Complexity and Change*. New York: The Free Press.

Schaeffer, F. (1982). Christian Faith and Human Rights. *Simon Greenleaf Law Review*, 2(5), 5.

Schein, E. H. (1997). *Organizational Culture and Leadership* (2nd ed.). San Francisco: Jossey-Bass Inc.

Schneider, J., & Littrell, R. F. (2003). Leadership Preferences of German and English Managers. *Journal of Management Development*, 22(2), 130-148 DOI: 10.1108/02621710310459694.

Schwarzkopf, H. N. (1992). *The Autobiography: It Doesn't Take a Hero*. New York: Bantam Books.

sec.gov. (2010). Retrieved June 7, 2014, from http://www.sec.gov/Archives/edgar/data/1001039/000119312510268910/d10k.htm.

Seidler-de Alwis, R., & Evi, H. (2008). The Use of Tacit Knowledge within Innovative Companies: Knowledge Management in Innovative Enterprises. *Journal of Knowledge Management*, 12(1), 133-147 DOI: 10.1108/13673270810852449.

Sendjaya, S., & Pekerti, A. (2010). Servant leadership as antecedent of trust in organizations. *Leadership & Organization Development Journal*, 643-663.

Severson, K. (2012, July 26). Chick-fil-A Thrust Back Into Spotlight On Gay Rights. *New York Times*, p. 13.

Shahin, A. I., & Wright, P. L. (2004). Leadership in the Context of Culture: an Egyptian Perspective. *Leadership & Organization Development Journal*, 25(6), 499-511 DOI:10.1108/01437730410556743.

Shamir, B., & Eilam, G. (2005). What's your story? A Life-Stories Approach to Authentic Leadership Development. *The Leadership Quarterly*, 16(3), 395-417.

Shillington, G. (2002). *Reading the Sacred Text: An Introduction to Biblical Studies*. New York: The Continuum International Publishing Group Ltd.

Simons, T. L. (1999). Behavioral Integrity as a Critical Ingredient for Transformational Leadership. *Journal of Organizational Change Management*, 12(2), 89-104 DOI: 10.1108/09534819910263640.

Slaughter, R. (1993). Futures Concepts. *Futures*, 25(3), 289-314.

Smith, D. (2001). *The Quotable Walt Disney*. New York: Disney Editions.

Stone, A. G., Russell, R. F., & Patterson, K. (2004). Transformational Versus Servant Leadership: A Difference in Leader Focus. *Leadership & Organization Development Journal*, 25(4), 349-361 DOI: 10.1108/01437730410538671.

Strategic Direction. (2008). Innovation is More Than Just a Good Idea: Creative Thinking + Strategic Leadership=Results. *Strategic Direction*, 24(8), 25-27 DOI: 10.1108/02580540810884638.

Szent-Gyorgyi, A. (1962). *QuotationsPage.com*. Retrieved August 20, 2013, from http://www.quotationspage.com/quotes/Albert_Szent-Gyorgyi/

References

Tabernero, C., Chambel, M. J., Curral, L., & Arana, J. M. (2009). The Role of Task-Oriented Versus Relationship-Oriented Leadership on Normative Contract and Group Performance. *Social Behavior and Personality: An International Journal,* 37(10), 1391-1404.

Taylor III, B. W. (1996). *Introduction to Management Science.* Saddle River: Prentice Hall.

The Denma Translation Group. (2003). *Sun Tzu: The Art of War.* Boston: Shambhala Publications Inc.

The Executive Fast Track. (2012). Retrieved November 1, 2012, from http://www.12manage.com/methods_mintzberg_ten_schools_of_tho ught.html

The Hindu. (2011, July 31). Retrieved August 1, 2011, from http://www.thehindu.com/news/national/article2311046.ece

The Strategy Institute of the Boston Consulting Group. (2001). *Clausewitz on Strategy.* (T. von Ghyczy, B. von Oetinger, & C. Bassford, Eds.) New York: John Wiley and Sons.

Thomas, B. (1994). *Walt Disney: An American Original.* New York: Disney Editions.

Tushman, M., & O'Reilly, C. (2002). *Winning through Innovation: A Practical Guide to Leading Organizational Change and Renewal.* Boston: Harvard University School Press.

Ulrich, D., & Ulrich, W. (2010). Creating Abundance. *Leadership Excellence,* 27(6), 8-9.

United Nations. (2006, June). *Support For the Formulation of National Sustainable Development Strategies in Pacific Small Island Developing States.* Retrieved January 21, 2012, from http://www.un.org/esa/sustdev/natlinfo/nsds/pacific_sids/solomon_isl ands.pdf

Utterback, J. (1996). *Mastering the Dynamics of Innovation.* Boston: Harvard University School Press. .

Vaitheeswaran, V. (2008). Innovation is More Than Just a Good Idea: Creative Thinking + Strategic Leadership=Results. *Strategic Direction,* 24(8), 25-27 DOI: 10.1108/02580540810884638.

van Woerkum, C., Aarts, M., & de Grip, K. (2007). Creativity, Planning and Organizational Change. *Journal of Organizational Change Management,* 20(6), 847-865 DOI: 10.1108/09534810710831055.

Vanderpyl, T. (2012). Rest is the Hidden Key to Successful Leadership. *Human Resource Management International Digest*, 20(7), 3-4.

Von Krogh, G., Ichijo, K., & Nonaka, I. (2000). *Enabling Knowledge Creation: How to Unlock the Mystery of Tacit Knowledge and Release the Power of Innovation*. Oxford: Oxford Press.

Washington, G. (1789). *The American Presidency Project*. (J. T. Woolley, & G. Peters, Editors) Retrieved February 25, 2012, from http://www.presidency.ucsb.edu/ws/?pid=25800

Watson, R. (2012). *Future Files: A Brief History of the Next 50 Years*. Boston: Nicholas Brealey Publishing.

Willard, D. (2002). *Renovation of the Heart: Putting on the Character of Christ*. Colorado Springs: NavPress.

Winston, B. (2002). *Be A Leader for God's Sake*. Virginia Beach: School of Global Leadership & Entrepreneurship.

Winston, B. E., & Patterson, K. (2006). An Integrative Definition of Leadership. *International Journal of Leadership Studies*, 1(2), 6-66.

Woll, T. (2002). *Publishing for Profit*. Chicago: Chicago Review Press.

Woolfe, L. (2002). *The Bible on Leadership : From Moses to Matthew Management Lessons for Contemporary Leaders*. New York: American Management Association.

World Vision. (2012). Retrieved November 12, 2012, from http://www.worldvision.org/content.nsf/about/history

Wren, D. A., & Bedeian, A. G. (2009). *The Evolution of Management Thought* (6th ed.). Hoboken, NJ: John Wiley & Sons, Inc.

Wuellner, F. S. (1998). *Feed My Shepherds: Spiritual Healing and Renwal for Those in Christian Leadership*. Nashville: Upper Room Books .

Yaprak, A., & Sheldon, K. T. (1984). Political Risk Management in Multinational Firms: An Integrative Approach. *Management Decision*, 22(6), 53.

Yukl, G. A. (2009). *Leadership in Organizations* (7 ed.). Englewood Cliffs, NJ: Prentice Hall.

Zachary, L. J. (2005). *Creating a Mentoring Culture: The Organization's Guide*. San Francisco: Emerald Group Publishing.

Zhang, Y., Goonetilleke, R. S., Plocher, T., & Liang, S.-F. M. (2004). *Time Orientation and Human Performance*. Hong Kong: Work with Computing Systems 2004 (Proceedings of the 7th International Conference).

References

Zweifel, T. D. (2003). *Culture Clash: Managing the Global High-Performance Team*. New York: Swiss Consulting Group Inc.

MORE BOOKS BY DR. DARRELL PARSONS

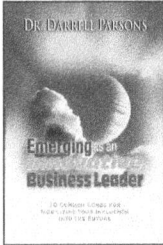

EMERGING AS AN INNOVATIVE BUSINESS LEADER
10 Common Cores for Mobilizing Your Influence into the Future
by Dr. Darrell J. Parsons

Out of the dust of failing organizations or fresh out of the halls of academia, a new breed of leader is emerging to take the reins in our world. Do you have the skillset you need to propel you into the the forefront of your world? From out of the myriad of research, Dr. Darrell Parsons concisely articulates ten of the most important competencies which are imperative for today's innovative leader. After reading this book, you will effectively be able add value to your organizaiton by choosing the innovative approach to company and personal development.
Hardback. ISBN: 9781602730854. $22.95 USD. 150 pages.
Tradepaper. ISBN: 9781602730748. $12.95 USD. 150 pages.

EMERGING AS AN INNOVATIVE CHRISTIAN LEADER
12 Common Cores for Mobilizing Your Influence into the Future
by Dr. Darrell J. Parsons

The kingdom of God is in need of innovative leaders which enhance or create value to their church, family, and life. With this understanding and biblical support, Dr. Parsons is able to concisely articulate twelve competencies which are imperative for today's innovative leader. When dealing with any group, emerging leaders can begin the process of leadership development by working on the competencies identified in this book. Included in the common core is leadership succession, ethics, rest and renewal, mentoring/discipling, trust, among others. Innovate your life today!
Tradepaper. ISBN: 9781602730656. $14.95 USD. 228 pages.

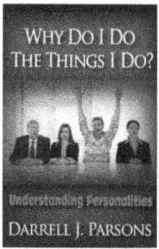

WHY DO I DO THE THINGS I DO?
Understanding Personalities
by Darrell J. Parsons

In this insightful book, Darrell Parsons identifies the four primary types of personalities and how they interact together. As you grow in understanding, you will gain the tools you need for developing successful relationships in all areas of your life. Tradepaper. ISBN: 9781602730199. $10.95 USD. Also, available in e-book formats.

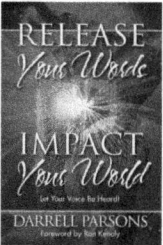

RELEASE YOUR WORDS—
IMPACT YOUR WORLD
by Darrell Parsons

Your words can make a difference! Treasures have been placed treasures inside you; learn to release them to influence your world. In this book, Darrell Parsons challenges you to use your voice to impact the world around you today.
Tradepaper. ISBN: 9781602730007. $9.95. Also, available in e-book formats.

AVAILABLE AT YOUR LOCAL BOOKSTORE OR ONLINE.

www.ingramcontent.com/pod-product-compliance
Lightning Source LLC
Chambersburg PA
CBHW050502190326
41458CB00005B/1394